# The emotional well-being of unaccompanied young people seeking asylum in the UK

# The emotional well-being of unaccompanied young people seeking asylum in the UK

Elaine Chase, Abigail Knight
and June Statham

Published by British Association
for Adoption and Fostering
(BAAF)
Saffron House
3rd Floor, 6–10 Kirby Street
London EC1N 8TS
www.baaf.org.uk

Charity registration 275689 (England & Wales)
and SC039337 (Scotland)

British Library Cataloguing in Publication Data
A catalogue record for this book is available
from the British Library

ISBN 978 1 905664 50 4

Project management by Miranda Davies, BAAF
Photograph on cover Justin Tallis/reportdigital.co.uk
Designed by Andrew Haig & Associates
Typeset by Avon DataSet Ltd, Bidford on Avon
Printed in Great Britain by Athenaeum Press
Trade distribution by Turnaround Publisher Services,
Unit 3, Olympia Trading Estate, Coburg Road,
London N22 6TZ

# Contents

Foreword
*Dr Sheila Shribman*                                                      ix

**1  Emotional well-being and mental health among refugee and
    asylum-seeking children and young people                             1**
Introduction                                                             1
Background literature                                                    2
Mental health among refugee and asylum-seeking young people             4
Social adjustment                                                        7
Relevant policy and legislation                                         9

**2  The study                                                         13**
Methodology                                                            13
Identification and selection of research participants                  15
Gathering information from young people                                18
Gathering information from professionals                               20
Analysis of data                                                       21
Characteristics of the young people in the study                       22

**3  Journeys and arrival in the UK                                    25**
The journey                                                            25
Arrival in the UK                                                       29

**4  Young people's experiences of good and poor emotional health      34**
Missing family                                                         34
Feeling alone                                                          36
Disturbed sleep                                                        37
Headaches and panic attacks                                            38
Depression                                                             39
Eating problems                                                        40
Anxiety                                                                40
More severe difficulties                                               41
Professional perspectives                                              43

**5  Young people's understandings of mental health and emotional
    well-being                                                         45**

**6  Experiences of primary care and other health services            51**
Experiences of GPs and primary care services                          51

Experiences of hospital-based and clinical services 56
Experiences of and responses to counselling services 58

**7   Being in care** **66**
Foster care 67
Informal or private fostering 72
Residential care 73
Semi-independent living 73
Independent living 74
Last resort accommodation 77
Young people's experiences of social workers 77
Age assessments 80
Finances and entitlements 83

**8   The impact of education** **87**
The wider benefits of learning 87
Barriers to education 92

**9   Experiences of immigration and legal services** **97**
Immigration status 97
Returning "home": identity and belonging 102
Legal and interpreting services 105

**10  Other sources of support** **109**
Religion and faith 109
Friends 110
Relatives 112
Community groups 113

**11  Resilience and the ways in which young people cope and adapt** **116**
Adapting to life in the UK 116
Ways of coping 122
Personal strength and resilience 125
Pregnancy and parenthood 127

**12  Conclusions** **131**
The significance of age, gender, ethnicity and country of origin 132
Impact of placement factors 134
Impact of other factors 135

**References** **139**

**Appendix: Study participants** **145**

## Acknowledgements

We gratefully acknowledge the financial support of the Department of Health (DH) for this study, although the views expressed in this report are those of the authors.

We would like to thank the director of children's services, the services manager, the team leaders and other staff of the social services department in the local authority participating in the study, as well as all other professionals and carers who gave it their time and support. Thanks also to Voice, in particular to Afsana Aramesh (specialist advocate), through whom we were able to identify other young people to take part, and to Youssouf Brahim and Mohammed who helped us so much in preparing and testing the research tools.

Our sincere thanks go to all members of the project advisory group who provided invaluable support to the study: Peter Aggleton (Thomas Coram Research Unit), Afsana Aramesh (Voice), Mano Candappa (Institute of Education), Joe Heatley (Home Office), Mathew Hodes (Imperial College, University of London), Bob Jezzard (formerly DH), Pauline Lane (Health for Asylum Seekers & Refugees Portal), John McCracken (DH), John Simmonds (BAAF), Jim Wade (University of York), Sandra Williams (DH), Morris Zwi (DH) and to Judith Dennis (Refugee Council) for technical support and advice. Thanks also go to Sharon Lawson for providing administrative support and to Marjorie Smith and Peter Aggleton for their editorial guidance.

Above all we would like to thank all of the children and young people who took part in this study and who were willing to share their experiences with us.

## Notes about the authors

**Elaine Chase** is a senior research officer at the Thomas Coram Research Unit (TCRU), at the Institute of Education, University of London. For the past 18 years, she has worked as a practitioner and researcher in public health and health promotion in the UK and internationally. The main focus of her work is on the well-being of children and young people experiencing particularly difficult circumstances and disadvantage.

**Abigail Knight** has been a researcher at the Institute of Education, University of London since 1995. Her research interests include the health and well-being of looked after children and young people, disabled children and their families, and children's rights.

**June Statham** is Professor of Education and Family Support at TCRU. She has nearly 30 years' experience of research on children's services and is particularly interested in support for vulnerable children and their families, including children in need in the community and children who are cared for away from home.

# Foreword

This exploratory study, which considers the wide range of factors that either promote or harm the emotional well-being of unaccompanied young people seeking asylum, raises important practice and policy issues for relevant services. Many of the findings will also lead to better understanding and the promotion of positive mental health among other groups of vulnerable young people.

The study is timely as it corresponds with the Government's commitment to improve the physical, mental and emotional health and well-being of children and young people from conception to adulthood – for children who are in relatively good health and those particularly vulnerable to poor health outcomes, as well as those who are ill. In my review of progress last year on the National Service Framework for Children, Young People and Maternity Services, I noted steady improvements in Child and Adolescent Mental Health Services (CAMHS) and a new emphasis on early intervention and prevention.

My department and the Department for Children, Schools and Families have commissioned an externally led CAMHS review which is looking at what progress has been made in delivering services to meet the educational, health and social care needs of children and young people at risk of and experiencing mental health problems. It will consider what remains to be delivered and how best this should be done.

Many of the young people that took part in this study had left behind very difficult situations and undertaken arduous journeys. It is heartening to see that many spoke of their joy and relief at being in Britain. We owe it to them to ensure that they receive the best possible care, based on a rigorous assessment of their needs, and best practice in delivery of appropriate services. This study is an important contribution to the debate, and I warmly commend it.

**Dr Sheila Shribman**
*National Clinical Director for Children and Young People and Maternity Services*
*Department of Health*
*May 2008*

# 1 Emotional well-being and mental health among refugee and asylum-seeking children and young people

## Introduction

In this book we present findings from an 18-month study (March 2006 to September 2007) conducted by the Thomas Coram Research Unit (at the Institute of Education, University of London) and supported by the Department of Health, which sought to examine the social functioning, emotional well-being and mental health of unaccompanied children and young people seeking asylum in the UK. The study took the form of an in-depth exploration in one London borough of the perspectives and experiences of children and young people seeking asylum, supplemented by interviews with key professionals with expertise and knowledge of working with this group. In addition, a small number of interviews were conducted with young people seeking asylum alone and accommodated in other London authorities. Although the research focused on the emotional well-being of young asylum seekers, many of the findings have relevance for understanding and promoting positive mental health among other groups of vulnerable or socially excluded young people.

In this opening chapter, we set the context and provide an overview of some of the key research that has been conducted concerning the emotional well-being and mental health of children and young people seeking asylum in the UK, either on their own or as members of families. In Chapter 2, we provide an overview of the aims and methodology of our study and give some background information about the young people who took part. Subsequent substantive chapters go on to present the findings from the research and demonstrate how various dimensions of the young people's asylum-seeking experiences affected their emotional well-being and mental health. The themes discussed, in order, are as follows:

- children and young people's journeys and arrival in the UK;
- young people's experiences of good and poor emotional health;
- young people's understandings of mental health and emotional well-being;
- young people's experiences of primary care and other health services;
- young people's experiences of social care services;
- young people's experiences of education services;
- young people's experiences of immigration and legal services;
- other sources of support that young people look to;
- resilience and the ways in which young people cope and adapt.

Each chapter concludes with a summary of points highlighting potential implications of the findings for policy and practice in relation to promoting the mental health and emotional well-being of unaccompanied children and young people seeking asylum. The final chapter summarises the main conclusions and revisits the original research questions.

## Background literature

Children and young people arriving alone to seek refuge far from their country of origin are not a new phenomenon. In the months leading up to the Second World War, the *Kindertransports* of Jewish children fleeing Nazi Germany and neighbouring countries are probably the most well-documented example. At that time, the British government gave permission for up to 10,000 children to enter Britain from all over Europe including Germany, Poland and Austria. Individuals ranged in age from three months to 17 years and arrived between December 1938 and September 1939 (Leverton and Lowensohn, 1990; Harris and Oppenheimer, 2002).

Central to children and young people's existence as "asylum-seekers" is the need to establish grounds for asylum or protection as enshrined in Article 1A (2) of the Refugee Convention (1951, amended in 1967). This defines a refugee as someone who:

> ... *owing to a well-founded fear of being persecuted for reasons of race, religion, nationality, membership of a particular social group or political opinion is outside the country of his nationality and is unable,*

*or, owing to such fear, is unwilling to avail himself of the protection of that country.*

Although there is no specific mention of children in the Refugee Convention, the United Nations High Commissioner for Refugees (UNHCR) Handbook (1992) does make it clear that the provisions of the Convention apply to people of all ages. Since 1987, the High Commissioner's Programme has highlighted the special circumstances of unaccompanied children and their need for both the determination of their immigration status and provision for their physical and emotional support.

UNHCR defines unaccompanied children as:

*... those who are separated from both parents and not being cared for by an adult who, by law or custom, has responsibility to do so.* (UNHCR, 1994)

In practice, they include:

- children who have become separated from their parents and have arrived in the UK by themselves;
- children who are being cared for by older siblings, distant relatives and family friends – people who would not by custom be their usual carers;
- children who arrive in the UK with family but whose care arrangements break down after arrival.

In the literature and in professional practice, the term "separated" is often used interchangeably with "unaccompanied" to describe children who arrive under the circumstances outlined above, although it has a different association for some organisations. For practical reasons, many agencies concerned with children's rights and well-being (e.g. Save the Children Fund and the Separated Children in Europe Programme) also adopt a broad view of "separated" children to encompass not only those who arrive alone in the UK, but also those who arrive "accompanied" but where the accompanying adult may not be able (or appropriate) to assume responsibility for the child once they have entered the UK.

For the whole of the year 2006, 23,520 asylum applications were received by the Home Office (Home Office, 2007). Out of these applications, 2,850 (about 12% of the total applications) were from unaccompanied asylum-seeking children and young people under the age of 18. In the same year, 2,565 initial decisions were made on asylum applications for unaccompanied minors. Of those decisions relating to children and young people aged 17 or younger (2,560), only seven per cent were granted asylum. A fraction of a per cent (only 10 applicants) was granted humanitarian protection, 22 per cent were refused, and the remainder (71%) were awarded discretionary leave, mostly up until their 18th birthdays (Home Office, 2007).

Within local authorities, social services departments (now children's services) have become the departments, by default, which have responsibility for the care of unaccompanied asylum-seeking children and young people. Children and young people under 18 arriving in the UK alone are entitled to protection under the Children Act (1989) and are supported by the relevant local authority and not directly by the Border and Immigration Agency (BIA), as is the case for adults.

## Mental health among refugee and asylum-seeking young people

The World Health Organisation defines health as 'a complete state of physical, mental and social well-being and not merely the absence of disease or infirmity' (WHO, 1978). In a US report from the Surgeon General's Office (USA Public Health Service, 2000) mental health is defined as 'the successful performance of mental function, resulting in productive activities, fulfilling relationships with other people, and the ability to adapt to change and cope with adversity'.

The mental health and emotional well-being of refugee and asylum-seeking children and young people have received increasing attention in recent years. However, most of the literature and research to date has been informed by clinical understandings of mental health, with relatively little attention paid to the broader aspects of emotional well-being. We briefly review the clinical literature relating to mental health among refugee and asylum-seeking children, and how this might be affected by age or gender, in order to provide a context for the more holistic understanding of mental health and well-being that informs the rest of this report.

The mental health difficulties or disorders most frequently identified among refugee children and young people by health professionals include post-traumatic stress disorder (PTSD), depression, anxiety, somatic conditions (physical symptoms with no apparent physical cause) and difficult behaviours, including aggression or disruptive behaviour. Up to 40 per cent of refugee and asylum-seeking children and young people may experience depression, PTSD and other anxiety-related problems that are serious enough to be classified as psychiatric disorders (Hodes, 1998, 2002a, 2002b).

From a clinical perspective, a wide variety of psychological instruments have been used to quantify the level of distress experienced by refugee and asylum-seeking populations. These are frequently designed to measure the extent of "trauma", "dysfunction", "difficulties", "anxiety", "depression" or "problem behaviour". Some measures are administered by mental health specialists others are self-reporting or are completed by caregivers or guardians, such as the Child Behavioural Checklist (Achenbach and Edelbrock, 1991; Bean et al, 2006). Several measures have been designed specifically to assess the effect of trauma, such as the Impact of Event Scale (Horowitz et al, 1979); the Child Post Traumatic Stress Reaction Index (CPTS-RI) (Frederick et al, 1992) and the Child PTSD Symptom Scale (CPSS) (Foa et al, 2001; Newman, 2002).

There is now substantial evidence which supports the cross-cultural validity of a diagnosis of PTSD (Hodes, 2000; Dyregov and Yule, 2006; Ethnolt and Yule, 2006). Research studies with children and young people exposed to war and organised violence in countries as diverse as Cambodia, Lebanon, Rwanda, Kuwait, Palestine, Afghanistan and Bosnia all demonstrate very similar responses to trauma among their study populations. Several studies have identified that girls are more commonly diagnosed with PTSD than boys (Green et al, 1991; Tousignant et al, 1999; Dyregov and Yule, 2006). Yet there is inconsistent evidence as to whether and how gender is a protective factor for children exposed to violence and trauma (Hodes, 2002b).

Based on previous research, there still remains an unclear relationship between post-traumatic reactions and age, and it is uncertain whether or not increasing age provides a degree of protection from the adverse effects of trauma. Dyregov and Yule (2006), for example, point to literature that shows a wide range of reactions to stress and trauma in children according to age and gender. Younger children present less "emotional numbing" but may present more overt aggression and destructiveness, and engage in repetitive play in which they re-enact traumatic events they have witnessed or experienced. There is some evidence to suggest that as children mature, increasing age may to some extent be a protective factor. For example, in a study of 48 unaccompanied asylum-seeking children and young people in Finland, Sourander (1998) identified that children under the age of 15 years presented with more severe psychiatric problems than those who were older than 15 years. Overall, though, there is some evidence to suggest that refugee children and young people may have better mental health outcomes than do adults exposed to trauma (Porter, 2005).

In addition to the range of measures applied to establish the extent of psychiatric difficulties experienced by refugee children and young people, other scales have been used to examine protective as well as difficulty factors in young people's lives. Probably the most widely administered and frequently used with refugee children and young people in the UK is the Strengths and Difficulties Questionnaire (Goodman, 1997; Fazel and Stein, 2003). These tools have been used to establish clear evidence that refugee children are far more likely than non-refugee children to experience mental health difficulties which impact on their social functioning outside of the clinical setting (Tousignant *et al*, 1999; Fazel and Stein, 2003).

These (and other) tools and measures derived from the disciplines of psychiatry and psychology have an important place in defining and establishing mental health needs, especially for clinical purposes. However, they may be limited in terms of what they contribute to our understanding of the contextual factors that might alleviate, or conversely exacerbate, clinical symptoms over a period of time. Porter (2005) notes how research on refugee mental health often accounts for psychopathology solely in terms of post-traumatic reaction to the acute stresses of war, conflict or other adversity. As such, high rates of psychological disturbance among refugees have been identified. However, relying solely on the use of psychological measures within a clinical context may fail to capture other important dimensions of the refugee experience that may be better articulated in a social rather than in a clinical context.

Once young people seeking asylum arrive within the host country, mental health problems associated with pre-flight experiences may be exacerbated by the lack of emotional or social support (Marriott, 2001; Stanley, 2001; Wade *et al*, 2005; Dyregov and Yule, 2006), by poor housing and accommodation and insecurity (Marriott, 2001) and by experiences of social exclusion or racism (Levenson and Sharma, 1999). There may be a propensity to attribute emotional or behavioural difficulties manifested by refugee children solely to trauma, when there are many other stress factors in their lives, such as uncertainty about the future, frequent moves, disruption of social networks, and language and cultural barriers that are likely to play a part (Vostanis, 2004).

Health and social services, in assessing and responding to the needs of refugee and asylum-seeking children, should be cognizant of how they can best promote emotional well-being as well as identify and treat more specialist mental health problems (Melzak and Avigad, 2005). Kohli and Mather (2003) refer to the need to promote the "psychosocial well-being" of refugee children, who may be in the process of assimilating and adapting to new social and cultural contexts. Services that can fulfil this function range from primary care and community-based services (including GPs, health visitors, teachers and other school staff), focused provision by social services and voluntary organisations, through to more specialist Tier-3 health services that provide specialist care and support for children and young people with severe depression or post-traumatic stress. In a small proportion of cases, asylum-seeking children and young people may require Tier-4 services, including hospitalisation in mental health units (Hodes, 2002).

## Social adjustment

With respect to social functioning and social adjustment of refugee and asylum-seeking young people on arriving in host countries, there is a developing literature that indicates the range of issues that affect positive as well as more problematic social adjustment. Resilience as a broad construct is frequently cited as a key prerequisite of good social functioning, with high levels of observed resilience associated with good social adjustment. Resilience has been defined in various ways but essentially identifies the ability to function competently despite living in or having lived in adversity (Schofield and Beek, 2005), the ability to sustain competence under pressure and normal development under difficult conditions (Gilligan, 2000; O'Dougherty *et al*, 2006) and the ability to sustain relative resistance to psychosocial risk experiences (Rutter, 1999).

Despite the evident anxiety, distress and trauma likely to have been experienced by refugee children and young people, there is a great deal of research that highlights their resilience and their ability to adjust to their new environments and circumstances (Kline and Mone, 2003; Kohli and Mather, 2003; Wallin and Ahlstrom, 2005). A common question raised in research is why some children and young people appear to respond and adapt better than others (Hodes, 2000) and there is a limited research literature on understanding how resilience is culturally influenced or interacts with cultural factors (O'Dougherty *et al*, 2006).

Rutter (2003) identifies a range of protective or mediating factors that appear to help refugee children overcome difficulties which may affect their psychological well-being. These include parents (or carers) who give full attention and good-quality child care; access to an extended family network or others who provide friendship and support in the community; understanding reasons for exile; permanent housing and permanent immigration status; maintaining links with their homeland; remembering good things about life in their home country; being happy in a new school; an ability to talk about stressful events; an ability to ask for help when things go wrong; hobbies and interests; high self-esteem and being optimistic about the future.

Research has begun to further elucidate some nuances in the social adjustment patterns of refugee children and young people. For example, the tendency of some refugee young people to function well in school in their host countries but to have greater difficulties with emotional and behavioural adjustment (see, for example, the work of Geltman *et al*, 2005); how gender and age on arrival impact on social adjustment (Rousseau *et al*, 1998; Cheung *et al*, 2000; Davies and Webb, 2000; Shaw, 2003); the intergenerational effects of refugee trauma and resettlement experiences (Spencer and Le, 2006) and the ways in which refugee young people strive to establish identities that can assist their integration and enable them to fit in (see, for example, Hymen *et al*, 2000; Sporton *et al*, 2006).

The degree of social, community and family cohesiveness enjoyed by refugee children and young people as well as shared values and belief systems have also been shown to have a key impact on resilience and provide protection to those previously exposed to trauma and adversity (Kohli and Mather, 2003; Shaw, 2003; Whittaker *et al*, 2005; Sporton *et al*, 2006). However, the ways in which shared community, social and religious values and belief systems mediate the effects of trauma remain unclear (Shaw, 2003).

Existing research concerned with the health and well-being of refugee and asylum-seeking children and young people has tended to consider them as a homogenous group. There is relatively little literature focusing on the specific needs of those children and young people who arrive on their own to seek asylum, or which attempts to disentangle the needs of different groups (for example, young men and young women or older and younger children) within the asylum-seeking population. The studies that have been conducted suggest that, overall, their mental health and emotional well-being needs (understood here in their broadest sense) are not well met by existing services. However, little research has attempted to understand, from the viewpoint of unaccompanied young people themselves, how their experiences of leaving their country of origin and seeking asylum in the UK have affected their emotional well-being, and how this in turn might shape the kind of help and support they need. This study aims to address that gap.

## Relevant policy and legislation

Over the last ten years, a number of government policies and programmes have gone some way in seeking to safeguard and support young people's physical, emotional, intellectual, social and economic well-being. *Every Child Matters* (Department for Education and Skills (DfES), 2004), the Children Act (2004), *Youth Matters* (2005), the *National Service Framework (NSF) for Children, Young People and Maternity Services* (2004), *Care Matters* (DfES, 2006) and *Care Matters: Time for Change*

(DfES, 2007) are all key components of the *Change for Children* national agenda in England. Together, these frameworks aim to ensure that local authorities and Primary Care Trusts (PCTs) can better support all children and young people in general, and provide tailored support to those facing difficult and challenging circumstances.

*Every Child Matters*, for example, seeks to ensure that all children and young people enjoy good physical and mental health and live a healthy lifestyle, that they stay safe and are protected from harm and neglect, that they get the most out of life and develop the skills needed for adulthood, that they are involved in and with communities and do not engage in anti-social or offending behaviour, and that they are not prevented by economic disadvantage from achieving their full potential in life. The Children Act 2004 provides the legislative backbone to *Every Child Matters,* and the *NSF for Children, Young People and Maternity Services* outlines a ten-year strategy to promote the health and well-being of children and young people that takes account of their individual needs and circumstances and which aims to achieve this through strengthening the integration of health, social care and education services.

*Care Matters: Transforming the lives of children and young people in care* (DfES, 2006) and *Care Matters: Time for change* (DfES, 2007) seek to improve outcomes for children and young people in and leaving local authority care. More specifically, they highlight that: local authorities and their partner agencies need to be better supported in their role as corporate parents; that children and young people, where possible, should be supported to stay in their own homes rather than be placed in care; and that they should be offered a greater choice of quality care placements and have access to the best possible education, health care and leisure activities. The Children (Leaving Care) Act (2000) is the legislative framework for supporting young people during their transition from care and stipulates the statutory obligations of local authorities in relation to young care leavers and determines their entitlement to leaving care support.

Young people seeking asylum alone in the UK who are under the age of 18 years, come under the care of the local authority in which they reside and as such are technically regarded as "looked after". While some local authorities have established separate and specialist asylum teams to support young people seeking asylum, others (especially where numbers are low) provide for asylum-seeking young people as part of generic children and young people's services.

In April 2007, the Government introduced the New Asylum Model (NAM) in an effort to speed up the processing of asylum claims and attempt to ensure that an initial decision is made on each claim within one month, and that any appeals on refused claims are concluded within five months. A process of case ownership was introduced which allocates a specific Border and Immigration Agency (BIA) official to each asylum claimant, who works with her or him from start to finish. In general, children claiming asylum pass through the NAM process in the same way as adults, and children over the age of 12 years who are claiming asylum in their own right undergo a full asylum interview. Under the NAM, case owners working with children receive specialist training to carry out their duties. The model also ends the discretionary leave awarded to young people with failed asylum claims once they reach the age of 17½ years.

A consultation paper, *Planning Better Outcomes and Support for Unaccompanied Asylum-seeking Children* (Home Office, 2007b) was issued by the Home Office in February 2007. This proposed a number of important changes to the asylum process for unaccompanied young people, including: the extended use of social workers to assess the age of young people; use of x-rays to determine the young person's age; ending the use of discretionary leave for children who are refused asylum; and working with overseas governments to make the necessary reception arrangements to return children whose claims are refused. It also proposed the identification of between 50 and 60 local authorities outside of the South-East of England where unaccompanied young people would be sent in the future, acknowledging the need to develop the expertise of these authorities (Immigration Law Practitioners' Association, 2007).

The proposals presented in *Planning Better Outcomes and Support for Unaccompanied Asylum-Seeking Children* stimulated extensive debate and discussion among organisations and agencies working with unaccompanied children and young people, with concerns expressed about their fairness and about the implications for the well-being of unaccompanied children and young people seeking asylum. An area of particular debate concerned age disputes, and research was undertaken (Crawley, 2007) that claimed to identify a range of inadequacies in the age assessment process. This work recommended that more young people should be given the "benefit of the doubt" as stated in Home Office policy; that independent (of the Border and Immigration Agency and social services) regional age assessment centres should be established; and that the age assessment process should be improved through guidance, training and support, thus ensuring a multi-agency approach which, it was hoped, would lead to consistent and better-informed outcomes for young people.

At the time of writing, the Government had just published the results of the *Planning Better Outcomes and Support* consultation and outlined its plans to implement reforms to the provision of support for unaccompanied children and young people in a new document: *Better Outcomes: The way forward – improving the care of unaccompanied asylum-seeking children* (Border and Immigration Agency, 2008). This document confirms the Government's plans to accommodate newly arrived unaccompanied asylum-seeking young people in authorities outside of London and the South-East of England and does indicate schemes to establish a number of specialist centres to ensure 'a consistent approach to age assessment'.

# 2  The study

The overall purpose of this study was to explore, from their own perspectives, the emotional well-being and social functioning of unaccompanied asylum-seeking young people in different living situations. It aimed to create insights into the types of social and health care programmes, actions and interventions that might positively impact on these dimensions of their health. The focus of the study was on obtaining a more nuanced and detailed understanding of the needs of unaccompanied young people seeking asylum, rather than evaluating or assessing the specific practice and approach of the hosting local authority with regard to supporting and working with this particular group of young people.

The main research questions we explored were:

- What factors are perceived to positively and/or negatively impact on the emotional well-being, social functioning and mental health of unaccompanied children and young people seeking asylum in the UK?
- Are there differences in emotional well-being and social functioning among unaccompanied children and young asylum seekers according to age, gender and their country of origin?
- What types of health and social care provision and services are useful in promoting their emotional well-being, social functioning and mental health?

## Methodology

Given that the focus of the study was on understanding the perceptions and experiences of young people, rather than on evaluating the specific services provided to them within the authorities in which they were accommodated, it was decided, in consultation with the project advisory group, to undertake the fieldwork in a single local authority with a high number of young people seeking asylum. A London authority was chosen, with specific expertise of working with unaccompanied children and young people seeking asylum. However, the large numbers of such children and young people accommodated within the authority, compared to other authorities, meant that there were additional pressures on local services to respond appropriately to very diverse needs. At the time of the research, a dedicated service to support the emotional well-being of unaccompanied children and young people had just begun operating in the authority and was funded for three years. This provided specialist support to young people with specific mental health needs, as well as capacity building and training for other professionals and practitioners within the local authority in relation to identifying and supporting the mental health needs of unaccompanied young people.

In order to provide some check on the "typicality" of young people seeking asylum in this one authority, additional research participants were identified through a national independent advocacy service offering specialist provision for unaccompanied asylum-seeking young people. A specialist advocate (working within this service) approached young people using the service, who met the selection criteria for the study, and asked them if they would like to participate. With the young people's permission, their contact details were then passed on to the research team. The young people seeking asylum who were identified through this route (approximately a fifth of the total sample) had experience of being looked after by a number of local authorities outside of the main authority hosting the research study.

After several meetings with the asylum services manager in the host authority to explain the nature of the study, permission to conduct it was given by the local Director of Children's Services. An ethical code of conduct was drawn up by the research team and subsequently also approved by the Director. Ethical approval was also obtained from the Local Research Ethics Committee (LREC) of the relevant PCT before interviewing health professionals in its employment.

Two important features of the research approach adopted in this study were that it allowed young people to decide what and how much information they shared with the researcher, and that it adopted a broad and holistic definition of "mental health". Young people were asked to talk about the things that made them feel well and happy, and the things that created difficulties for them or made them feel sad. The avoidance of terms such as "mental health" or "mental health difficulties" was intentional and enabled many young people to talk openly about their lives and well-being from a holistic perspective. Where young people themselves introduced words such as "mental" health or associated terms such as "depression", "stress", or "trauma", the researcher would discuss these in more depth. Young people therefore led the direction of the discussion, and primacy has been given to their perceptions and understanding of what they felt promoted or negatively affected their emotional well-being. There were many instances where young people were clearly selecting the information they chose to share with the interviewer – a perfectly normal response for young people meeting researchers on only one or two occasions. Despite this, the level and detail of their narratives and the accounts they gave of their lives were strikingly detailed. Young people were quite clear when they reached a point in a narrative where they did not want to continue. This would be indicated with phrases like, 'I don't want to talk about that', 'That is in the past now', 'I want to forget that' or 'I don't remember what happened then'. Experiences prior to arrival in the UK, both in their countries of origin and throughout their journeys, were only explored to the extent that participants were comfortable to talk about them. This inevitably resulted in variation in the level of detail provided and in the topics that young people chose to focus on in their discussions with the researcher.

## Identification and selection of research participants

The majority of young people who took part in the study were recruited through the social services department of the host authority. The three specialist teams working with unaccompanied children and young people – the children's asylum team, the youth asylum team and the transition team (working with young people aged 18 years and over) – were provided, by the researchers, with information drawn up after meetings and discussion with each team, to guide them in identifying the young people who would be invited to participate in the study. It was explained to practitioners that it was important to include young people with a range of experiences in terms of their transition to life in the UK, the extent to which they appeared to be coping with various aspects of their lives here and the extent to which they had been known to experience mental health difficulties.

The selection of the young people through the different asylum teams ensured that a proportion would be in foster care placements (those from the children's asylum team), a proportion would be in semi-independent accommodation (particularly those supported by the youth asylum team) and the remainder would be in independent accommodation (particularly those who were 18 years and over). This approach also ensured that children and young people from a range of ages were included in the study. Practitioners were also asked to consider the gender and country of origin of those whom they identified to take part, so that the cultural and ethnic backgrounds of the young people they were most likely to be working with were included in the study. The final sample provided a good balance of different placement types, ages, gender and countries of origin.

As stated earlier, about 20 per cent of the young people were identified through an independent advocacy service that worked with asylum-seeking children and young people across a number of local authorities. In addition, within the hosting local authority, three young people no longer directly supported by the authority were identified through local voluntary sector agencies including the YMCA and a children's rights organisation.

In order to work within data protection guidelines and to protect young people's confidentiality, a protocol was agreed whereby social workers and key workers first approached young people to ask if they would like to participate in the study. A simple information leaflet about the study was prepared by the researchers and translated into 12 different languages reflecting those most widely spoken in the young people's countries of origin, including Pashtu, Dari, Farsi, Mandarin, Cantonese, Portuguese, Amharic, Kurdish Sorani, Arabic, French and Somali. This leaflet was made available to the children's services teams in the host authority as well as to local voluntary organisations and other agencies likely to come into contact with young people seeking asylum. Once the aims of the research were explained to young people, they were asked whether they were still happy to take part in the research. If they agreed, their contact details were passed on to members of the research team who then made direct contact with the young person. For children in foster placements, the procedure for accessing asylum-seeking children included an additional stage, since it was necessary for the researchers to liaise first of all with the allocated social worker and then with the foster carer before direct contact could be made with the child.

The final sample consisted of 54 young people aged nine to 23 years. Forty-four of them were from the participating local authority which, as of September 2006, had 1,112 young asylum seekers registered as looked after under three age-specific asylum teams. In total, the details of 75 young people within the hosting authority were passed on to the research team. The remaining 31 who did not take part either chose not to participate, repeatedly refused to answer messages or calls made by the interviewer, or their contact details were no longer valid. (This happened on several occasions with young people who were 18 years and older and for whom no alternative contact details were available.) Of the 10 young people approached from other authorities in London and elsewhere through the specialist advocacy service, none declined to take part once they had been contacted by the interviewer.

Informed consent was given verbally by all the young people participating in the study. It was decided not to ask for their written consent since this would unnecessarily over-bureaucratise the research process. Given that all the young participants were frequently subjected to procedural and bureaucratic immigration processes, it was felt important to make the distinction between these statutory requirements of them and the voluntary nature of their participation in the research.

Because they were identified through gatekeepers, it is possible that the asylum-seeking young people taking part may have particular characteristics, for example, being more fluent in English, coping better with their situation or being less likely to be critical of the provision made for them by the local authority. However, when compared to the overall population of unaccompanied asylum-seeking young people within the hosting authority, a good match was achieved in terms of the age range and countries of origin of the participants. The final sample did include more young women than young men. Although this does not entirely match the overall gender pattern of young people within the hosting authority (of which between 40 and 45 per cent are female within the 16–17 and 18-and-over age groups), this is more likely to reflect an observed greater willingness of the young women to take part in the research compared to the young men who were invited to participate. Furthermore, the feedback from young people concerning the social work practice they had observed and experienced was very variable in terms of how positively or negatively it was viewed. Although not a random sample, the young people participating in the study nevertheless reflected a breadth of experience and have generated rich data in terms of the range of factors which either promoted or negatively affected their emotional well-being.

## Gathering information from young people

When young people were met or spoken to for the first time, they were asked whether or not they would like to have an interpreter present. In most cases, they chose not to do this and preferred to speak in English, even if they struggled to some extent to express themselves. Time was allowed in the research process to enable them to speak as freely as possible. The only participants who chose to have an interpreter present were two young women who were Chinese and spoke Mandarin. This said, having the main aims and objectives of the research in their own language through the translated information sheet was very helpful for some young people – particularly those who had not spent a very long time in the UK. Overall, researchers were struck by the high level of English language acquisition that most young people had accomplished since arriving in the UK, and the degree of fluency with which they spoke.

Young people were asked to talk about their experiences since coming to the UK and to focus on the things that had made them feel well and happy since arriving here and the things that had made them feel sad or had created difficulties for them. A topic guide was used to draw out key aspects of young people's lives and experiences. This covered the following aspects of their migration and settlement:

- the journey;
- arrival in the UK;
- access and use of services including social services, primary care, legal support;
- education;

- placements;
- friendships and social networks;
- affiliation to church, other religious and/or community groups;
- links and contact with family members;
- sources of support;
- eating habits and diet;
- hobbies and interests;
- immigration status;
- any other aspects of their lives that they felt were important to discuss.

Discussions with young people lasted from about 45 minutes to three hours. The researchers frequently met a young person on more than one occasion, for example, an initial conversation in a neutral venue such as a café followed by a more in-depth interview at a later date, and this was sometimes supplemented by additional telephone discussions. In total, more than 80 interactions took place between the researchers and the young people taking part in the study. Detailed notes were made of initial introductory meetings, and all substantial interviews (the main discussion with each young person) were recorded using a digital recorder or tape recorder and then transcribed.

A further dimension to the research methodology was to offer young people the opportunity to document aspects of their current lives using a disposable camera. Eight chose to use this method, and it proved to be a successful way of facilitating discussion about their experiences. Young people were invited to take pictures of things, people or places that had positive and negative associations for them. The researcher had the film developed and the pictures were then used to promote discussion about their emotional well-being. Importantly, the interpretation of each photograph was provided by the young person in response to questions asked by the researcher, such as 'Can you tell me about this picture?', 'Who is in this picture?', 'Where is this place?', 'Why did you decide to take this picture?', etc. A further benefit derived from offering young people the use of a disposable camera was that researchers had an opportunity to meet them more than once, allowing a familiarity and rapport to be established. This proved beneficial even when young people who had expressed an interest in using the camera later decided, after meeting the researcher, that they would prefer to just have a discussion. The opportunity to meet young people on more than one occasion undoubtedly added to the richness and quality of the data.

Young people were often reminded throughout the research interaction that they could withdraw from the research at any time or refuse to answer any of the questions posed by the researcher. Where young people became distressed in the course of the discussion with the researcher, it was temporarily halted and only resumed if and when the young person was happy to proceed. Young people were always asked whether they would like to be referred for further support or advice. A line of referral was established prior to the commencement of the research between the research team and the team managers within the relevant social services asylum teams responsible for the young people participating in the study.

## Gathering information from professionals

Professionals and practitioners were selected to take part in the study through a process of identifying, through initial key contacts and available documentation, plus an element of "snowballing", those within the local authority who were known to be working closely with children and young people seeking asylum.

The total of 31 professionals and carers interviewed, included foster carers of children or young people participating in the study (3); social work team managers (4); social workers (5); support workers and personal advisers within the asylum team (3); residential care managers and residential support workers (4); primary mental health workers – both in voluntary and statutory agencies (2); a specialist CAMHS worker (1); general practitioner and nurse practitioners (3); specialist looked after children's nurse (1); educational psychologist (1); children's rights officers (2); specialist asylum youth worker (1); youth offending service manager (1). In addition, meetings were held with all four asylum teams as a whole to introduce the study. These also provided early insights into the key issues that were perceived to affect the emotional well-being of unaccompanied children and young people seeking asylum.

Interviews with key professionals working with young asylum seekers in various services of the participating local authority were conducted using a semi-structured interview schedule. This included questions relating to the common concerns and issues with regard to young people's emotional well-being and mental health; any differences in terms of emotional well-being observed in relation to age, gender and ethnicity; the ways in which children and young people communicated issues related to their emotional well-being and mental health; perceptions of who young people looked to for support; the extent to which placement factors positively or negatively impacted on emotional well-being; perceptions of other social, economic, legal, educational, spiritual and health factors that might promote or hinder young people's emotional well-being; the types of indicators that practitioners looked out for to signify that young people required more specialist mental health service intervention; and any perceived gaps in services to support the emotional well-being of children and young people seeking asylum in the UK. The majority of interviews with professionals and practitioners were conducted face to face with a small number carried out over the phone. Interviews with professionals lasted for an average of one hour. All interviews were recorded using a digital recorder or tape recorder and transcribed.

## Analysis of data

Once all data from the research interviews had been transcribed, a thematic analysis was conducted using the constant comparative method (Glaser and Strauss, 1967) to identify recurrent themes. Emerging themes were then checked for "negative instances", or examples which contradicted these themes (Merriam, 2002; Seale, 2002), prior to their inclusion in the findings. A one-page summary of key factors was compiled for each young person, including information on current age, age on arrival, country of origin, gender, level of education and placement history. This was used to facilitate the analysis of core demographic data. The transcripts from interviews with young people and notes from interviews with professionals were scrutinised to draw up a list of key themes. These themes were then used to develop a grid for subsequent analysis of transcripts, with any new emerging themes added to the grid as the analysis proceeded.

The focus of the analysis was on the meanings and understandings which young people themselves attributed to emotional health and mental well-being, and their own perceptions of how these were reflected in the approaches of the professionals providing services. This study is thus intended to complement, rather than duplicate, more clinically-focused analyses of the mental and emotional health of unaccompanied young people seeking asylum, such as those described in the introductory sections of this report.

## Characteristics of the young people in the study

Figure 1 shows the age of young people at the time of their arrival in the UK. Boys and young men participating in the study were more likely to have arrived at a younger age than their female counterparts. This finding reflects the pattern of arrival at a national level whereby more boys and young men come to the UK than girls and young women, with boys tending to arrive at a younger age. National data for unaccompanied children and young people are grouped into three age ranges: under 14; 14 and 15; and 16 and 17 years. As is the case nationally, the largest proportion of the study sample was in the 16 and 17 year age group on arrival

*Figure 1*
**Age on arrival of young people participating in study**

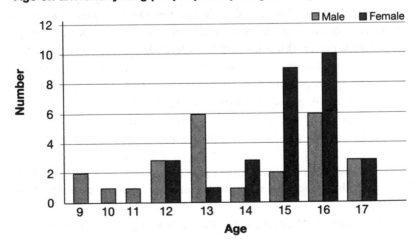

(40%). Among the study sample, slightly more young people arrived aged under 14 than in the age group 14–15 years, whereas in the national figures for young people entering the country alone each year, there are normally fewer children in the under-14 age group than in the 14–15 age group (Home Office, 2007).

Figure 2 (below) shows the age of young people at the time of their participation in the study; most of them were aged 18 years or over. This is in keeping with the numbers of young people supported by the local authority within this age group, which were almost double the number of young people supported by the youth asylum team (16 and 17 years old) and the children's asylum team (under 16 years). This also matches the national pattern of age distribution of unaccompanied minors, whereby the majority of local authorities currently support more young people in the 18+ age group than in other groups.

Young people in the study came from a total of 18 different countries: Eritrea, Ethiopia, Afghanistan, China, Nigeria, Democratic Republic of Congo (DRC), Somalia, Iran, Angola, Cameroon, Rwanda, Burundi, Liberia, Chad, Albania, Pakistan, Syria and Uganda. The largest number of participants came from Afghanistan (9); Eritrea (7); Ethiopia (6);

*Figure 2*
**Age of young people when participating in study**

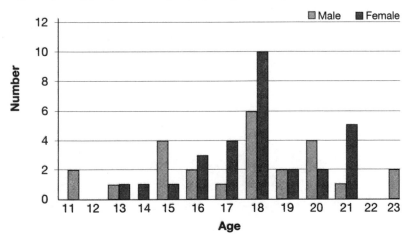

Nigeria (5); China (4) and Somalia (3). National data for the first quarter of 2007 showed that the most frequent countries of origin for unaccompanied young people were Afghanistan, Iran, China, Somalia and Eritrea (Home Office, 2007). The study sample therefore was fairly well matched with national patterns of unaccompanied young people entering the UK, although only two young people from Iran took part.

There was a difference in the balance of boys and girls according to the country they arrived from. For example, all participants from Afghanistan were boys, while all those from Ethiopia, Eritrea and China were girls.

Most young people travelled to the UK with some kind of intermediary or agent and often reported being unaware that they were being taken to England. The agents were normally paid by surviving parents or other adults who took responsibility for children and young people if their parents were dead or missing. An agent would either see them onto a plane or into the back of a lorry or travel with them and then "disappear" at the airport or port of arrival. Young people were sometimes, though not always, briefed on where they should go in the airport or port and were advised to say that they were seeking asylum. Some young people talked of travelling with someone that they knew. This person would pay their fare and, like the agents, disappear once they arrived. These people were variably described as 'good Samaritans', 'nuns', Jehovah's Witnesses or in the case of one young person, her employer (a British person working in her country and for whom she had provided child care). It is important to note that, while a number of professionals indicated that there was evidence that some of the young people they worked with may have been trafficked to the UK, none of the children and young people we spoke to raised this as an issue in our discussions with them. Consequently, trafficking was not an aspect of migration that we were able to explore in this current study.

## Arrival in the UK

Whatever young people encountered on their journeys to the UK, their arrival in England was for many of them a complete shock. They often described being catapulted into a world that held nothing familiar. Aliva, aged 17 when she arrived from Somalia, said it was like 'being dropped somewhere in the ocean'. Alban, who was 15 when he arrived from Albania, said:

*I didn't speak any English so it felt like I was coming to a different planet, really. I hadn't seen any big buildings, I was only used to a small town.*

Zalmai, 11 years old when he arrived from Afghanistan, said:

*I was so nervous being somewhere with people I didn't know and I couldn't speak the language.*

Ajani, also from Afghanistan and aged 14 on arrival, commented:

*I was tired, frightened. I had not slept for three or four nights and had not eaten.*

The reception they received at airports and ports was frequently described as hostile and uncaring. After her terrifying journey, Nadine described being met:

*The lady was really horrible, she was really horrible and then the man came and started, like, feeling sorry for me 'cos I was like very starved. Like for about almost 48 hours, I didn't have anything to eat and I was just feeling dizzy and, oh, it was just terrible, and then the man said, 'Just give her a break.' And then they took my picture and they took my picture that came out as though I was something – like a criminal – I always look back at this picture and think, 'Oh my God, is this me?'*

Sherriff was 16 when he arrived in the UK from Liberia. He described how his lack of literacy skills made it very difficult for him to answer the questions he was asked:

*They were asking me questions, you know, 'How did you come here? What flight did you enter?' Because when I was in Liberia I didn't know how to read . . . I didn't know how to, you know . . . I could speak a little bit English, but they was asking me what flight do you enter and that was difficult.*

Many young people discovered that when they first arrived they were not believed by immigration officials who met them. Zemar arrived at Heathrow airport from Afghanistan when he was 16 years old. While he was relieved to have landed after a very difficult journey, he was shocked at his reception:

*They locked me in a room from 8am in the morning. They took fingerprints and at 8pm they told me to go out and come back at 9am in the morning. I said, 'Where shall I go?'*

Zemar stayed in the airport until it closed and then spent several hours on the streets outside the airport until it re-opened in the early hours of the morning. Later that morning he was questioned further and asked for either a Pashtu or Dari interpreter since he was fluent in both languages. The interpreter told him, 'You are lying. You are not from Afghanistan – swear on your mother's life that you are from Afghanistan.' Zemar's anger was evident as he recounted this event:

> *When I get here I haven't slept for 72 hours and I am 16 years old . . . And when I arrive, instead of asking me 'Have you eaten? Have you slept?' you are asking me to swear on my mother's life . . . a mother who I couldn't even say goodbye to when I was leaving.*

Mesaret arrived from Ethiopia when she was 16 years old and was left at the Immigration and Nationality Directorate office in Croydon (now the Border and Immigration Agency (BIA)) by the person who brought her to England. She received very little support initially from either voluntary organisations or the children's services department to which she was sent. She ended up alone on the street when all the offices were closed and was taken in by an Amharic-speaking woman who looked after her for the night and the next day took her back to the voluntary organisation where she had sought help. During this time Mesaret described feeling very frightened, abandoned and disappointed at the way she was treated: 'I was crying the whole day'.

Many others described a mixture of relief that they had arrived safely in the UK but also fear about what to expect. When Patrick arrived from the DRC aged 12, he said he had no idea whether or not it was legal to beat children.

Arrival in the UK was evidently more complicated and difficult for those young people in their mid- to late teens. Younger children seemed to receive more immediate support from children's services and their age was not questioned. When Ruth, now 13½ years, arrived from Eritrea at the age of 12, she described how, despite being very frightened and confused and not speaking any English, the police and other authorities were 'nice to me'.

For older children who arrived in their mid- to late teens, having their age disputed was not uncommon. In total, about a quarter of the young people we spoke to had had their ages disputed – either at the point of entry into the country or at a later date while under the care of a children's services department. Age disputes were lengthy processes which were frequently described as being intrusive and degrading and are discussed later in Chapter 7. The anxieties and stress caused by age disputes when young people first arrived was evident from their descriptions. A number of them talked of their dismay at not being believed by the BIA or children's services departments and not being listened to.

Maryam, who came aged 17 from Iran, described having her age disputed on arrival and as a result was sent to stay in an adult hostel provided by the BIA:

*It was a huge place with thousands of people there from everywhere. It was horrible. I remember. I never want to think about it, it was just not nice. I have really bad memories.*

Similarly, Betania from Angola, aged 16 when she arrived, was not believed:

*I found it so difficult because everything was so negative to me at the time. I didn't know why. Like I didn't know what I was supposed to say when I came here and I did not know also why they didn't believe me. They put me in a hotel and then I went to court – they called me for interview. After a month they wrote to me saying that my claim was refused and then after six months I went to court and they dismissed my case. They still did not accept my age.*

As a result, Betania was "dispersed"* to another authority. She later returned to the original authority, sleeping on friends' floors and working illegally to survive. She did this for two years.

A failed age dispute meant that several young people were detained here in the UK. For most, this was just for a short period of time but for

---

* The Immigration and Asylum Act 1999 introduced a national dispersal policy for asylum seekers through which they are moved to local authorities away from London and Kent in order to ease pressure on these authorities.

Mahamat, who arrived aged 17 from Chad, it meant several months in two different detention centres from which he was told he would be deported. Having experienced a period of incarceration back in Chad, this experience was particularly traumatic for him. A last-minute appeal clarified the fact that the decision to deport him had been made on the basis of a very poorly translated statement (see later section on solicitors and interpreters). On appeal, not only was he able to stay in the UK but was granted indefinite leave to remain.

---

### Implications for policy and practice

- The circumstances surrounding each asylum-seeking young person's departure from their home country and the journeys they make to come to the UK are unique and need to be treated as such.
- Many, though not all, young people seeking asylum have experienced extreme trauma and distress before leaving their countries or during their journeys.
- Young people seeking asylum in the UK may have left their country of origin at a young age and have faced accumulated loss of family members over many years.
- Age disputes on arrival in the UK cause significant distress for young people (see further discussion in Chapter 7).

# 4  Young people's experiences of good and poor emotional health

As will be discussed later on in the report, it was striking how well many young people were able to function and cope on a day-to-day basis and to achieve remarkable things, despite the levels of adversity they had experienced. This said, the majority of children and young people we spoke to indicated some degree of emotional distress. Their descriptions of the types of emotional difficulties they faced from day to day are discussed further in this chapter.

Often the first indications of a young person's overall emotional well-being emerged some way into the research interaction. There were numerous occasions where young people began participating in the research in quite a guarded way but gradually talked more and more openly about their experiences. Young men in particular sometimes gave the impression of being very in control, and could appear quite brusque at an initial meeting. Through the course of their participation in the research, however, many disclosed quite severe anxieties, feelings of isolation, fear and loneliness. Young men as well as young women often cried during the discussions with the researchers – some were striking in the way they vacillated between being very tearful and laughing out loud. The spectrum of emotional difficulties they described was very wide and ranged from disturbed sleep patterns to severe mental illness which had required medical intervention and sometimes even hospitalisation.

## Missing family

Missing family members and either grieving their loss (if they had died) or constantly wondering about whether or not they were alive was a recurrent theme. General anxieties about what was still happening in home countries and whether remaining family members were safe were also common. Even those who knew their families' whereabouts missed them a great deal. Some young people described how they could not face using the tracing system of the International Red Cross to try and find missing relatives, since they preferred to think that there was some hope that they were still alive. Mahlet explained:

*My social worker keep asking me to find my father [her only remaining relative] but I don't want to know . . . Maybe they are going to tell me bad news – I don't want . . . now I am just hoping that he is alive and maybe somewhere.*

Fifteen-year-old Ali, when asked about things that made him sad, said:

*First of all my family. My mum, dad and brother are back in Afghanistan so I can't see them or talk to them about anything. So that's one of the most difficult things.*

Zemar, now aged 21, from Afghanistan, reflected:

*Not seeing my family is the most shocking thing. I know that even when I grow so old, and my eyebrows turn white, I will still picture my mum, you know – that warmth that you feel is unprecedented, it is unmatchable – you can never match that with anything.*

William, who had arrived from the DRC aged 17, powerfully described in detail the day that his mother and sister died and the impact this had on him:

*And what happened one day, I was taking shower . . . we had like a shower outside. Some guns just start, 'cos where I was living, gun machine you can hear it everywhere, every time. And I didn't know it was happening in my house and I just hide. When it finished, it cool down and everything quiet. I could hear people running up and down. I came inside the room and I find my sister dead, my mum dead . . . and my young brother was crying there. And I bite my tongue; I thought I was dreaming.*

Since arriving in the UK, William had also learned of the death of his father. He described how he frequently felt despair about the total loss of his family but said he talked to no one:

*I am not that kind of person to tell everyone what's happened 'cos it's paining me – I can't talk about it. I don't want to talk. When I find myself alone it's paining me . . . seeing people with their family. I don't have anyone. I feel lonely. Sometimes I'm here crying myself. It's not good at all, it's not nice . . . asking God, 'Why?, why?, why?' I was too young to lose all my family. Why?*

## Feeling alone

Not being able to talk about feelings with anyone was common. Young people often described even limiting what they talked about to their friends. A number of professionals also commented to us on the frequency with which they felt young people were masking and hiding how they were really feeling. Many professionals also felt that young men were less open about their feelings than young women, who on the whole tended to have access to more peer support networks. One mental health worker with a voluntary organisation felt that young women's greater readiness to disclose their emotional difficulties meant that they were more likely to get support earlier. Young men, on the other hand, were more likely to reach a crisis point before seeking help.

Feeling 'alone', 'having no one', 'having no family' or seeking replacements for family – 'God is my family now' – commonly emerged from young people's descriptions of their feelings. They talked of a variety of ways in which they tried to cope and deal with this sense of loneliness. Many young men and women intimated that they hid their loneliness and sense of sadness "behind closed doors" – crying alone. Seeking distractions from their feelings was another very common coping strategy.

Some attributed their isolation to where they were living and a perceived lack of community or sense of caring. Simeon, aged 20 when we spoke to him, having arrived from Somalia when he was 13 years old, was living in a flat in a tower block. He described his feelings of isolation:

*It makes you sad. This type of environment is not good for anyone. Everyone keeps to themselves. I have no choice but to keep to myself and to think, 'Why are they like this?' No one talks to no one. I'm not the sort of person to walk past someone in trouble, like an old lady getting attacked. Everyone's a victim here. The only time I feel good is when my friends come round. I enjoy cooking, watching TV. But it doesn't suit my personality [living here]. I went to a community meeting on the estate but no one spoke about how bad the estate is. Someone got shot outside the block one year ago – I heard the bullet. People just don't care.*

Houmam described how, after six months of being here, he still felt alone outside of school time and during the weekends and holidays. 'I go out on my own. I go to the park. When I go, I just sit and think.' Similarly, Mesaret, aged 18 and from Ethiopia commented, 'I feel isolated. I travel a lot' (i.e. to reduce the feelings of isolation).

## Disturbed sleep

Not sleeping, disturbed sleep, nightmares and dreams were also indicators of distress commonly described. Nadine from Rwanda, now aged 19, said:

*I started adapting a little bit. But then at night I would have, like, really strange dreams and stuff and sometimes I wouldn't sleep at all. I would just say I don't really want to sleep. I don't know what happened to my parents, are they dead or something.*

During an initial meeting with 17-year-old Kenneh from Liberia, he recounted in some depth the repeated nightmares that he had of being chased and how even during the day he sometimes thought he recognised the faces of his pursuers in the security guards of the local shopping centre close to where he was now living.

Mesaret from Ethiopia linked her poor sleeping to her depression and to fears related to things that had happened to her before:

*I'm quite depressed. I don't always leave my room. I don't have good sleep. Things make me wake up – I have bad dreams and anything small outside can wake me up. I get up really tired for school. Sometimes I sleep with my light on – if I have bad dreams, I don't want to be in the dark. In [her previous accommodation] the girl upstairs was very heavy footed. I kept thinking someone was coming in.*

Alban talked of his frequent nightmares about having to return to his country. He said: 'I wake up in the morning and am relieved I'm still here.'

Going to sleep with the television, radio or light on, or taking sleeping tablets to help sleep, were common responses for some young people. Sometimes sleep difficulties manifested as periodic bouts of insomnia followed by intervals when young people could sleep quite well. Sixteen-year-old Houmam described how he did not have nightmares but could just not get to sleep and would watch television all night, a problem that he had never experienced before coming to the UK. Ruth, aged 13 from Eritrea, said she had to sleep with the television on because before coming here her mother would always sit with her before she went to sleep. The links between disturbed sleep and poor mental health were well understood. In the words of Ibrahim: 'I can't sleep and if I can't sleep it makes me crazy.'

## Headaches and panic attacks

Having headaches was a very common symptom described by young people. Aliya (now 21) described how she still has regular headaches and nightmares about the events that she had experienced. She managed the headaches by taking the maximum dose of paracetemol almost every day. She knew from her course in health and social care that she shouldn't be taking medication as regularly as this but said, 'I can't function without it now. I'm addicted.'

Similarly, Mahlet said that she only visited her GP when her medication for "migraine" ran out. The headaches began after her mother died (Mahlet had witnessed the beating that led to her mother's death). She found that the medicine worked after two or three hours if she rested.

Panic attacks were also alluded to by several young people. Ibrahim commented, 'I am on the bus and I'm thinking too much and I have to breathe fast.' Alban, who arrived aged 15 from Albania, described frequent panic attacks which sometimes woke him up at night. Remi, 16 years old, also talked of how she sometimes panicked when faced with having to go to a meeting or specific event: 'I feel panic a lot and stress a lot.'

## Depression

Depression was often mentioned or described by the young asylum seekers we spoke to, again particularly those in the older age group. Some alluded to 'depression' in their narratives of what made them feel happy, or conversely what made them feel sad or unhappy. When Maryam was asked to describe what she had referred to as her 'depression' she said:

> *It usually starts with laziness – I just want to sleep for 12 hours a day. And I get really upset about things that aren't meant to hurt you; I make things bigger than they are.*

Nadine also described a similar sense of inertia and tiredness:

> *I had another stage of depression – I couldn't get out of my bed and my foster carer [the depression started while she was in foster care] would always call me in the morning and say, 'You know, you have to put yourself together – this is not the end.'*

Zemar from Afghanistan reflected on how his occasional sense of despair was nothing compared to what he knew others suffered:

> *There are days when you hate going outside your bed, you hate the walls, you hate people. For me it was short term but for others it takes their life away. They suffer so much degradation and they lose humanity for themselves; they lose all respect for themselves and others.*

Rakeb experienced severe bouts of depression at times and was constantly on medication to alleviate her symptoms. Her depression was sometimes overwhelming: 'Sometimes I just feel to die . . . I don't want to continue any more.'

Chrisna described what she referred to as 'changes of mood'. She attributed this to her personal problems which she felt made her behave in this way. She was aware that she tended to take her anger out on those close to her, like her boyfriend, but that her anger was not really directed at them.

## Eating problems

A number of young people described difficulties with food – either losing their appetite or eating too much and having problems controlling their weight. Chrisna, when asked about her health more generally, said:

> *It's up and down really. I mostly lose weight. It's about not eating and about stressing. I don't eat enough. I don't eat healthily as well.*

Malashu also described how she had trouble eating. She had tried to raise this as a problem with her social worker whose response had been: 'Well, you should eat' . . . 'and they wrote it down and that was it.' Malashu emphasised: 'I wasn't happy . . . that's what I was telling them.'

## Anxiety

High levels of anxiety that young people lived with most of the time were also common. Mahlet's description of her feelings was similar to feelings expressed by others:

> *I'm just thinking about all the things . . . like my head is going. I am thinking that my head is going to explode because I'm just thinking.*

Other anxieties related to not feeling completely safe. For some young people, these feelings abated over time, for others they remained. Ajani described how after about six months he began to feel safe: 'No one can touch us now.' Mahlet, on the other hand, did not always feel safe:

> *Sometimes I don't feel safe . . . sometimes I just feel what if someone is coming in here to kill me [she explained that her social worker never calls and her key worker comes once a week] . . . they never know what happens in, like, five days.*

Mahlet's fears related to the fact that her mother had been killed for political reasons and her father was missing. She thought that the people responsible might also come looking for her because she had information they might want.

Professionals working in general practice commented that young people feeling unsafe was a common expression of anxiety. These concerns were often linked to their housing situation. Kiki from Eritrea commented that she sometimes felt unsafe living with only one other young woman in hostel-type accommodation where all the other living space was occupied by young men and bathroom and kitchen facilities were shared. A specialist nurse adviser in general practice recounted how she had worked with two sisters from Iraq who had arrived on their own in the UK. One of the sisters had previously been imprisoned where she had been repeatedly raped. On arrival she was placed in a hostel with men, where washing and cooking facilities were shared, and was so traumatised that she was unable to ever take a bath or shower.

Other manifestations of distress, particularly in younger children, appeared to be more temporary and reportedly subsided once they were reassured and cared for by others. Not surprisingly, it appeared easier for children in foster placements, given the right care and support, to cope better with the changes and turmoil they experienced. For example, Zalmai's foster mother said:

*He used to cry all the time – he was missing his mum. I used to hug him and say, 'I'm your mum now.'*

Similarly, 15-year-old Ali from Afghanistan felt that his isolation for the first few months was linked to not being able to speak English and not having anyone to talk to. As he learned more English, life became easier for him. Ajani, also from Afghanistan, described a time when he would just cry in his room alone for long periods of time, but this changed once he was reunited with his older brother (they met each other again in a local Hindu temple).

## More severe difficulties

A few young people (6) described retrospectively how they had experienced severe mental health difficulties ranging from extreme memory loss, repeated attempts at suicide, episodes of psychosis (where they heard voices) and acute depression. In total, four young people talked of attempts at suicide or to self-harm. Joy, aged 17, who had come from

Nigeria when she was 13, described taking some drugs, she said, more in an effort to be listened to than anything else. A young man called Innocent, also from Nigeria, had made several unsuccessful attempts to end his life, ending up in a psychiatric unit each time.

Some mental health difficulties pre-dated young people's arrival in the UK. Innocent's first attempt at suicide, which he attributed to the death of various members of his family, happened at home in Nigeria. He described the death of his mother and father, killed in their church because they were minority Christians in a predominantly Muslim part of the country. Innocent had not told anyone about this when he arrived in the UK where a second suicide attempt was also hidden from health professionals. However, subsequent breakdowns led to his being detained a number of times under the Mental Health Act (1983) and he had spent several periods in hospital.

### Age

A significant factor affecting the type and extent of emotional distress presented by young people in our study was age. There was a clear difference between younger children and those who were older in terms of their apparent level of distress. When asked about whether there was anything that made them unhappy or sad, several of the younger children said that there was nothing. When 11-year-old Namir asserted, 'I am a happy person,' this characteristic was confirmed by his foster carer who described him as having a sweet, happy and good-natured personality and temperament.

Children entering the UK at a younger age often found it easier to adapt to a new culture and learn English. Those arriving aged 16 and 17, for example, had far less time to become established in their new environment before having to make fresh applications to the BIA to remain in the country. They frequently described having simultaneously to cope with a series of major issues such as placement moves, remaining in education, sorting out their legal situation and taking exams. A specialist nurse for looked after children observed:

*For me, it always seems to be the ones that come into the country when they are older that struggle the most. They don't have that time to be*

*cosseted, everything happens all at the same time and they've got*
*something like a year or two years where they are not in school, don't*
*know the language . . . it's harder to learn the language when you're*
*older.*

There was no doubt about the connection between the ongoing anxieties
experienced by young people and their immigration status. Older young
people nearing the end of their discretionary leave period, those in the
process of making a claim for extended leave to remain and those
applying through the appeals process to overturn a refusal to remain were
more likely to describe or present symptoms of severe emotional distress
or anxiety through the course of the research discussion.

## Professional perspectives

The aspects of mental health and emotional well-being observed by the
professionals we spoke to closely mirrored those described by young
people. However, professionals tended to report on them in different
ways, using more clinical terminology, such as "bereavement reactions"
or "adjustment disorders".

Professionals gave examples of the types of behaviours that triggered
their concerns about the well-being of particular young people who were
seeking asylum. One social worker described a young woman who always
dressed like a man and wore a cap. Gradually, it became apparent through
working with her that she had been violently raped in her country and
dressed in this way to avoid attracting any male attention. Another young
person had suddenly shaved off all her hair and was struggling with drug
use problems. One young man was self-harming – cutting his hand – and
this was noticed by chance when he came to collect his allowance from
the social services department, although the social worker noted that it
could just as easily have been overlooked.

A mental health worker from a specialist voluntary agency providing
ESOL (English language support) alongside emotional and other practical
support for young people when they first arrive in the UK talked about the
high levels of need that she encountered. She commonly met young
people who were self-harming, had attempted suicide and had difficulties

43

with food and eating that were linked to high levels of depression and anxiety.

---

**Implications for policy and practice**

- In a largely opportunistic sample of 54 unaccompanied young people seeking asylum, a very wide spectrum of difficulties in emotional well-being was observed and described by young people.
- Young men tended to be less likely than young women to talk about or seek advice and support for emotional difficulties that they were facing.
- Older participants were more likely to express feelings of anxiety than the younger children.
- Older young people appeared to be more likely to experience the types of stresses and anxieties that can exacerbate other emotional health problems.

---

# 5 Young people's understandings of mental health and emotional well-being

This chapter examines how young people seeking asylum understood notions of mental health and its positioning in their lives. The study was guided by a holistic approach to mental health and emotional well-being, and we were interested in how young people described, articulated and communicated aspects of their well-being which were not physical. As discussed earlier, the term "mental health" was not directly used with young people, and they were asked instead about the things that made them feel well and happy, and the things that made them feel sad or created difficulties for them. It is worth noting that, although there were specific reasons for adopting this approach with young asylum seekers, research has shown that young people in general often do not relate to terms such as "mental health", and fail to perceive this as relevant to their own lives (Armstrong *et al*, 2000; Harden *et al*, 2001).

Sometimes, however, young people in our study used terms that enabled the emotional and mental health aspects of their lives to be looked at more specifically, but still from the young person's perspective. Such triggers for discussion included terms which had no clinical connotation such as "sad", "not comfortable", "worried", "stressed" or conversely being "happy", "peaceful" or "comfortable". Alternatively, other terms denoted a more clinical and diagnostic understanding of the state of their mental health, and were perhaps expressions they had learned through talking to other young people or professionals who had worked with them. These included terms such as "depressed", "traumatised" or others which indicated self-harm, for instance, "do something to myself" or, more openly, "tried to suicide".

Other allusions to mental health difficulties centred around trouble concentrating as a result of preoccupation with other anxieties and problems. Ibrahim described this as:

*The brain is, you know, small because it is thinking, thinking, finished . . . there is no power there.*

William from the DRC talked of how he had chosen a more vocational course in catering rather than information technology which, he felt, would require more focus and attention. He said:

*But my head is already damaged to be concentrated to something like [ICT] you know? But if I give myself I'll do it, but it's, like, I am not going to have enough time 'cos I think a lot, I think a lot, a lot, a lot.*

It was common for young people to describe 'thinking too much' about things that had happened, about things back home and frequently about what would or might happen depending on the outcome of their asylum applications. The most common ways of dealing with 'thinking too much' was to attempt to find distractions and other ways of coping. These are discussed further in Chapter 11.

A common theme was that young people often did not identify with what might be thought of as western notions of treating emotional difficulties as a mental health issue. Participants often situated their emotional responses to the various traumas and experiences they had encountered in their "heart", and were at times perplexed by the suggestion that these responses should be addressed through the "mind".

Ibrahim from Pakistan said: 'You have the thinking and it is in the heart.' Similarly, Mahamat from Chad described how he could not understand why he was offered medication for his feelings of depression. He described the loss and sadness that he was feeling as 'a sickness of the heart, not of the mind'.

Mahlet from Ethiopia explained this clearly when she said:

*I think the counsellor thinks that if you are speaking it, it just goes away but it doesn't . . . it's not in your mouth and like you took it out – it's inside in your heart . . . so you can't take it out. I just told you now but it's still inside me . . . I got it in here [motions to her heart], it doesn't go out.*

There were particular concerns and issues for young people about the associations of "mental", which they understood to mean being "out of control", "crazy", "talking out loud" or "hearing things". (Similar understandings have been demonstrated among children and young people in general, e.g. Roose and John, 2003; Street *et al*, 2005). An understanding of mental health which encompassed both positive and negative attributes was not something that was generally well understood by the young people we spoke to. At the time of the research, Aliya from Somalia was completing an access to nursing course. She talked about how she had only come to fully understand the term "mental health" through a recent session on the course. It was a new concept to her that an understanding of mental health could incorporate positive aspects of feeling well, attached, happy and balanced on the one hand, and negative feelings of, for example, sadness, loneliness and anxiety, on the other.

Mahlet commented that she had refused counselling when offered it because:

*I don't want it . . . I felt like they just make you crazy – they just treat you like a crazy person, like you are just losing your mind or that kind of thing.*

A social work team leader also highlighted these evident differences in what was understood by "mental health":

*I definitely sense a cultural view of what mental health and counselling is . . . there's definitely a lack of understanding of what we call counselling in the West and what the process is.*

One GP interviewed, who had many young patients who were seeking asylum, talked of the complexities of language use. In his view, it was not just a matter of young people not having the English words to express feelings and symptoms, but the fact that the type of language used to describe health was so different in other cultures. He gave examples of how, in some cultures, colour is used to denote the level or type of pain experienced, for example, a "red" pain would denote a hot or burning pain. He also felt that many "psychological issues" are explained in physical terms through the use of phrases like 'I have pain all over, doctor', which might be an indirect way of saying they are "depressed". He felt there was a general reluctance to talk to a doctor about anything that was not physical and commented:

> *One of them [young person seeking asylum] once described to me that a doctor is for sorting out your physical problems, not for sorting out your brain.*

The aversion to counselling and other talking therapies (discussed further in the next chapter) expressed by many young people in our study can thus partly be explained by the associations that "mental health" and mental health-related services had for them. This is clearly illustrated by the following discussion between the researcher and Claude from Burundi, in which Claude explained why he did not want to ask for counselling:

C: *It's different here . . . everything when you say you are stressed, they going to say you are mental . . . something like that . . . For me it's shit. I don't like someone to call me mental. Mental is one who become like crazy or can't think, who fight you if you move close . . . This is the one we call mental. Even like counselling, they may think I'm mental. That's why I don't like to use those types of services because I don't want anyone to say I'm mental . . . 'cos I don't think I'm mental.*

R: *I don't think they would call you mental . . .*

C: *Is it? [seems surprised] Because the way I hear on the radio or read in the newspaper is that if someone is stressed or have anorexia, they call it mental, mental, mental.*

R: *Well, what they say is that people have mental health problems or difficulties.*

C: *Yeah, mental health problems . . . that is what make me feel like . . . because when they going to write, they going to write you got mental health problems, isn't it?*

He continued:

C: *Sometimes I think to talk about it will cause more problems because,*

*like now yeah? The way we talk . . . my body start to feel sad,*
*something like that.*

R: *I'm sorry Claude. Do you want to stop talking now?*

C: *No, I'm saying the way I feel, I feel emotional . . . something like*
*that . . . I don't know why.*

A few young people spoke about what would happen in their own countries if someone became mentally unwell or emotionally disturbed. Mahlet talked of how people with evident mental health difficulties would be taken to the church and baptised with holy water (in Ethiopia). Nadine told about how the idea of sitting down and talking about your problems was completely alien to "African" culture:

*In Africa, if you have a problem, there is no way that you are going to*
*see someone who is going to tell you, 'How are you feeling today?' In*
*Africa, it's like you kinda just have to let everything go or just keep it*
*locked in because there is no form of saying how you are feeling.*

Sherriff from Liberia had experienced severe mental health difficulties since arriving in the UK. He felt that if this had happened in his own country, he would have been treated far worse than he had been treated here:

*When I was in Liberia, I didn't know about that, I didn't . . . maybe*
*someone is crazy . . . or he maybe crazy but there is nobody willing to*
*help you. Maybe you can be on the streets looking for food or looking*
*for somewhere to sleep or something like that. And everybody would*
*be running for you. But when I came here, I thank God that I see*
*someone who is really skilled for that.*

## Implications for policy and practice

- Beliefs about and understandings of emotional well-being and mental health commonly held in the UK are different in many ways to those understood by young people coming from other countries and cultures to seek asylum – although some understandings, such as negative associations with the term "mental", may hinder young people of all backgrounds from seeking or accepting help.
- Young people seeking asylum sometimes come from cultures where the concept of focusing services and therapies specifically on emotions and feelings is very alien.
- The language that has evolved in many western countries in relation to mental well-being is not well understood by many children and young people arriving from other cultures.
- There is an evident need to try to formulate and promote a language for emotional well-being and mental health that is less stigmatised and better understood by young people from a range of cultures.

# 6 Experiences of primary care and other health services

In this chapter, we discuss young people's experiences and responses to primary care and other services they have come into contact with in connection with their emotional well-being and mental health, including hospital-based, clinical and counselling services. Some of the difficulties that young people seeking asylum described with respect to engaging with primary care and other health services resonate with difficulties reported in research on access to health care among looked after children and young people more generally.

## Experiences of GPs and primary care services

The interactions that young people seeking asylum recounted of general practice were quite mixed, involving both positive and negative experiences.

Aliya, aged 21 and from Somalia, described the difficulties and frustrations she had experienced and the fact that she felt that her GP would not listen to her. With her first GP, she had tried to explain that she had sustained a head injury during the events prior to coming to the UK. He had prescribed anti-depressants which made her feel very sick and unwell. She had also asked him if she could have a full check-up (including a blood test), only to be told that this was not necessary. During the course of the research discussion, Aliya alluded to very traumatising events that she had experienced on her journey via Kenya to the UK – events which she was unable to talk about but the memories of which were visibly distressing for her. It appeared to the researcher that she was linking the need for a "blood test" to the traumatic events that she had experienced:

> *And I am worried about my health, because I never had a full check-up and I might be suffering from something that I don't know. I have this thing – I know I shouldn't worry because I know I'm healthy – but*

*I have like a skin thing and my skin itches . . . I ask him [GP], 'Can I have a full check-up?' and he says, 'You don't need it.'*

Aliya summed up her experiences of two GPs as 'they don't listen'. Other young people also talked of difficulties in actually registering to see any doctor. Others still had concerns about how the GP would respond to their anxieties. Chrisna explained that she had not told her GP about her sleeping problems since she was concerned about being prescribed something she would become 'addicted to'. She said she knew of lots of people who had sleeping difficulties and ended up being addicted to their medication.

Faith, aged 17, from Nigeria, felt that the medication prescribed by the GP for her headaches had not helped. She commented that the doctor had not asked her about her feelings and emotions at the time when she went to see him about the headaches.

Professionals who participated in the research also commented on the fact that young people were frequently taking medication for physical or emotional symptoms. One mental health worker in a voluntary organisation working with unaccompanied young people seeking asylum estimated that about 80 per cent of those she saw were on some form of medication, either to help them sleep or to reduce their symptoms of depression.

Claude from Burundi went on to outline some of the difficulties he anticipated in trying to talk to a GP about his feelings – something that he was not used to doing. He also alluded to the fact that medication was, he felt, unlikely to help him:

*I don't know if I can talk to a doctor, I don't know what gonna happen 'cos I got no idea really. I haven't tried. I don't even know if I can go to doctor and tell him I'm not feeling well . . . How can I start? And even I think there is no need to go there just 'cos there is no medicine you can take to make you feel well, is it?*

Other reservations about accessing GP services centred on confusion about what the GP or general practice nurse could do to "help" young people. One specialist nurse for looked after children (LAC) felt that the

GPs themselves similarly felt unsure about their role in relation to this specific group:

> *I don't get the impression that young people know what the GP is and I don't think GPs know what to do with these young people. I think there is a lot of stigma around asylum-seeking children and asylum seekers so they don't have the best experiences when they go to community settings and health settings. I think maybe they don't use them.*

Similarly, a nurse practitioner in one general practice who worked extensively with young people seeking asylum commented:

> *Practices like this are few and far between. I often wonder how people would be received if they tried to register at a standard GP practice. Some would be brilliant and others . . . It's too variable, there's no standard of how someone might be received or treated.*

Mesaret, aged 18 and from Ethiopia, talked quite positively about how her GP had referred her to counselling, especially in relation to the difficulties she was facing in 'getting along with people'. She explained that she felt that some young people found her strange and that she was aware that she was impatient with others. The counsellor had discussed strategies to help her, for example, explaining to others that she did not feel like talking. The GP had also respected her wishes not to take medication because 'I don't want to get addicted to tablets'.

Zemar commented positively on the fact that his GP was not British but from Africa, which meant that 'he was different – he could connect to me, he was so sensitive'. Zemar speculated that his GP may well have been a refugee himself and that this might explain how he could connect with him. He said: 'I thought, "this is one of us".'

Those working in general practice described the difficulties of knowing where to refer young people who were experiencing severe mental health difficulties. The local Child and Adolescent Mental Health Service (CAMHS) had limited capacity. There was also a feeling that there was limited specialist knowledge and expertise for supporting this particular group of children and young people. Social care practitioners within the local authority in which the research was conducted, and who were working with children placed in foster care in many different local authorities, commented on the variability of the quality of care that children with specific needs were able to access through local CAMHS services.

The GPs and other health workers interviewed for this study all had substantial experience of working with unaccompanied young people seeking asylum, but they expressed some concerns that other practices might be far less well equipped to support their specific needs. Significantly, at least two other practices within the local authority that were approached to participate in the research study declined on the grounds that that they did not have enough knowledge of this area of work. A GP from one of the practices that did participate commented:

> *That would be good to explore further. Does that mean that other general practitioners are not coming into contact with them [asylum-seeking young people] or not recognising that they are coming into contact with them?*

A number of health and social care professionals discussed some of the complexities of identifying and making appropriate referrals when they felt that asylum-seeking young people were manifesting quite severe mental health difficulties. The types of indicators that they reported looking out for included eating problems, how young people presented themselves, issues around budgeting and difficulties in orientating themselves to new situations. Generally, it was felt that there was quite a high level of resistance among some young people seeking asylum to receiving any specialist professional help and a need for services to find ways to engage better with those who may resist this type of support.

Social care professionals also talked about the struggles they encountered in registering young people with GPs and in accessing other related services such as interpreters. A team leader in one of the social services asylum teams talked of how distressing it was for one pregnant young woman to go through labour soon after arriving in the UK, with doctors making decisions for her, and not understanding what was happening.

Some social care professionals identified the particular problems that arose when young people were kept in detention centres, and thought that there was a lack of communication between immigration services, detention centres and the children's services department. They reported that this made it very hard to support some young people with quite severe emotional problems.

Within the local authority hosting the research, a specialist service had been set up as a time-limited project to help build local capacity to support the emotional well-being and mental health of children and young people seeking asylum. Professionals within the children's services department valued the expertise that the project brought to this area of work, and the scope for referral and advice if and when they had concerns about a particular young person's well-being. However, once the funding terminated, the local CAMHS would have to take over provision of direct support to young people. One consultant with CAMHS indicated that this would be "a shock" to the service, since it lacked the capacity and resources to meet the range and specific needs of asylum-seeking young people.

A specialist nurse for LAC within the local authority commented about the lack of training for professionals specifically in relation to mental health:

> *We aren't trained completely in this area – unless you have a nursing background in that particular area [mental health]. Even doing training with us would help so that we can pick up on even more of the problems . . . Of course [it would help] only if there is a service to refer these issues on to.*

More generally, there was a view widely held by professionals that there needed to be more possibilities for referral into mental health services that were specific to the needs of asylum-seeking young people. In particular, there was a perceived lack of appropriate services for older young people (aged 18+) who technically should be transferred to adult mental health services at this age. One nurse practitioner identified the lack of referral opportunities for this age group as a significant gap in services:

*This is a huge issue about services not allowing for that transition [from child to adult mental health services]. The problem is that you and I know that there is no cut-off point from child to adulthood; we have to help that transition and be in constant contact with all the other people involved. It's a big gap, a nonsense . . . What happens between 18 and 21? This is the argument about people feeling that they are just being dumped when someone should just care what happens.*

## Experiences of hospital-based and clinical services

A small number of young people – about six of the 54 in the study – talked about their experiences of either Tier-3 clinical mental health services or hospitalisation as a result of their mental health difficulties. For some, hospitalisation occurred soon after their arrival as a means to alleviate severe symptoms of trauma. Kenneh, for example, arrived from Liberia when he was almost 14 years old. He was very mentally unwell as a result of experiencing severe trauma. He said that he was hospitalised for two or three days during which he was given medication to 'put me to sleep'. After that time he said that he was allowed to leave the hospital and subsequently took medication for two or three weeks, after which he was 'OK'. He explained that he then had some 'lessons' although he did not describe what these entailed (presumably some kind of counselling or psychotherapy). He commented: 'I don't think they understood the illness well.'

Innocent from Nigeria similarly found his experiences in hospital unhelpful. He found the doctors in hospital rude to him and stayed only for a very short period of time. However, he did say he had benefited from a community-based counselling service through which he saw his counsellor once a week.

Ibrahim similarly described how he could not see the benefit of going to hospital for his mental health difficulties and clearly did not understand the rationale for his treatment regime or the side effects of the drugs he had been prescribed by hospital doctors:

I: *I have mental health problems and I am going to hospital and now I am not going because I said I don't want to go there because you know*

> *they are giving me tablets – 30 mg every day – and they said you need to eat with this. I said, 'When I eat this [the tablets] I can't sleep, so why take this tablet?'*

R: *Have they said what the problem is?*

I: *They have said you have a depression. Then they give me this [showed several boxes of different tablets]. I don't understand . . . this is for sleeping . . . but when I wake up I don't feel very good. Doctor has given me this . . . my health is all gone. When I came to this country I was healthy and had power . . . now I am not. I don't have power. I can't do anything. The brain is, you know, small because it is thinking, thinking, finished. There is no power there.*

In contrast, some young people accessing clinical mental health services indicated that therapeutic services had helped them a great deal in coming to terms both with what had happened in the past and with what was happening to them currently in the UK. At times, the relationship built with a mental health specialist was key to a young person's well-being. Rakeb, for example, had suffered memory loss as a result of the various traumas she had experienced. Although she continued to experience extreme bouts of depression, the psychiatric support she received over a number of years from the same psychologist had proved essential for her:

> *For me, my psychologist was like part of my family because, first, I was growing up in her hands and second, she put everything back inside me which I losted [sic]. I lost my personality, I lost my memory, I lost my confidence for a while and she put everything back inside. She took me back to my personality, to my qualities inside me . . . All of me is back.*

Twenty-one-year-old Sherriff, who arrived from Liberia at the age of 16, was living in a supported housing unit at the time of the research and had spent periods of time in hospital due to severe mental health difficulties. He described how he had symptoms of psychosis – 'I was hearing voices' – and found the experience of being hospitalised very frightening. This said, he recognised the benefits of having had the medical support and of his continuing medication which he knew kept him well.

R: *And now, looking back, do you think it helped you to be in the hospital?*

S: *Yeah, well I was supposed to be in hospital. I wish I did be in hospital, you know, look after me. Maybe I can be on the streets you know, or do what I am not supposed to do, you know, or suicide. Be in hospital they assess me and then they give me medication and I take it . . . It help me.*

## Experiences of and responses to counselling services

A review of studies reporting children's views on mental health services has suggested that there is greater ambivalence among "vulnerable" children and young people (those who were looked after, adopted or had experienced abuse) than among children in the general population towards using mental health services, and in particular an ambivalence about talking about their feelings (Davies and Wright, 2008).

Many, though not all, of the young people to whom we spoke had been offered some form of "counselling service". Some had tried to attend counselling sessions but had stopped after one or two. Several issues emerged from young people's narratives in relation to counselling and similar therapies which might help to explain this aversion.

Firstly, there was a commonly shared view that counselling meant talking about what had happened to them in their lives, events associated with trauma and crisis, and that this process was in some way expected to help them forget or erase the negative experiences that they had endured. However, many of those who had tried counselling felt that the recounting of the events had not helped but had the adverse effect of making them remember trauma more clearly, making them sad or unable to then function or focus in a way that they wanted. Sebel's response to counselling, along with those of other young people in our study, may indicate that counselling alone was not the most appropriate intervention for her and that a more specialist approach was required. Aged 18 and originally from Ethiopia, she had arrived in the UK when she was 16 years old. She had moved from Ethiopia as a young child, then to Yemen and later Dubai with her mother, from whom she was later separated. Before fleeing

Dubai and coming to England, she had been subjected to repeated sexual abuse. Her account of her counselling experience was similar to that of others we spoke to:

> *Every time I came from there [counselling] I am just crying and crying, remembering things . . . the lady was really lovely but it wasn't helping.*

Sebel said that she would rather keep busy, do things, talk to friends and go to church. At the time of the research, she had not seen a counsellor for more than a year.

Nanu, aged 20 and from Eritrea, said that she had tried counselling but that talking about what had happened to her didn't make her forget. She also felt she would rather do things that kept her busy:

> *For me, the better things helped me is that I go to college . . . that help me a lot. I used to concentrate on my study and forget everything. I just want to be someone for me and my son. When I stay at home, all I think about is family, myself and what I have been through, these problems. But now I have college, I think about what I am going to do next year, what's my progress now . . .*

Joy, now aged 17, commented that she was offered counselling but:

> *I didn't go 'cos I'm . . . there's no point me talking to a counsellor 'cos it not going to change anything is it – just talking?*

Secondly, there was the fact that counselling required young people to talk to strangers – people with whom they had no kinship or tribal ties – about their lives and experiences. Counselling was often offered to young people soon after they arrived in the UK, at a time when they were having to "tell their story" to different officials and often had no clear understanding of the roles and responsibilities of the various organisations and agencies with which they came into contact. One GP who provided a service for many young people seeking asylum commented on the stigma associated with asking for help about your mind:

*For most of them that [an invitation to go for counselling] means, 'You think I'm a nutter,' . . . or it equals weakness or not being dependable.*

Several health professionals noted the frequency with which young people presented with generalised symptoms such as fatigue, headaches and body aches, abdominal or chest pains, which had no apparent physiological cause. Although they would not make an appointment to talk about the emotional side to their health, if these physical symptoms were treated with respect (even when there was no physiological explanation for them), young people would sometimes begin to talk about other concerns in their lives.

Another barrier to the take-up of counselling was that young asylum seekers sometimes assumed that their experiences were so far removed from those to whom they would be talking that it would be impossible for others to understand. When asked why she had not considered going to speak to her doctor about her feelings of depression, Nadine explained:

*Because I just . . . they, like, they wouldn't deal with my problems you know. They can't help me . . . they don't . . . I just . . . they just wouldn't understand how I am feeling. I just think the way I am feeling is just too much for them to handle . . . so you know, I just say that I won't even bother you. I will just do it [deal with it] myself.*

This said, Nadine later intimated in the discussion that she was worried about her feelings and thought that she probably did need some sort of help. When, after over an hour, she was asked if she still had time to carry on talking, she said:

*I am really free today 'cos I was saying I would really like to reveal how I am feeling . . . 'cos this is like relieving me for today as well and I said [to myself], at least I can say I had a really long chat and I say how I am feeling.*

When asked whether there were other people she could talk to, Nadine continued:

*No, not really. I would not go into as much detail like this. I would just say something on the surface and just keep quiet. So, maybe one day I will just have to go for counselling because if this carries on any longer . . . I always fear for myself. I am like . . . imagine if I just lost it, you know. So I think to myself, maybe I shouldn't be so . . . maybe I should tell the social services that I want counselling, you know.*

A number of professionals thought asylum-seeking young people could benefit positively from more informal types of counselling and support. In particular, the ways in which staff worked with children in a residential unit for unaccompanied young people was thought to be very positive. One GP commented:

*I think in the homes they do a lot of counselling but it's done very low key – you know, they talk things through with staff and gradually get bits, more and more and more.*

The manager of one residential unit for unaccompanied children verified this point:

*We have staff here who speak the languages and are mature. The young people see them as substitute parents, which helps and works very well since we can get to the underlying issues. We can do more than counselling because we are with them 24/7.*

Research more generally on what children and young people say they want from mental health services certainly indicates that what matters most to them is staff who are approachable, non-judgemental and empathetic (Armstrong *et al*, 2000; Harden *et al*, 2001; Buston, 2002; Gibson and Possami, 2002; Street, 2004). Those working closely with young people may well be able to develop supportive relationships that enable them to begin to explore difficult emotional issues, and to identify when they need additional help. However, when professionals did not have the same degree of day-to-day contact with asylum-seeking children and young people as, say, residential care staff, it may be more difficult to identify any additional mental health support needs.

Some young people had never been offered counselling but felt that they would have benefited from it. Betania was 18 years old at the time of the research, but had had her age disputed when she arrived in the UK from Angola at the age of 16. Since she was deemed to be older than she said she was, it seemed that she had not been offered emotional support. She had tried to tell the authorities about what had happened to her in Angola and that she needed some help:

*I had some serious problems and I told them when I came here and they didn't listen to me.*

Zemar talked of his experience of using a telephone counselling service because he was too embarrassed to go and meet anyone face-to-face. However, after confiding in one of his teachers at college, he was persuaded that rather than go to counselling, he should 'get involved socially and broaden my network of socialisation, rather than just relying on one helpline'. Zemar thought that had been good advice for him.

Some young people spoke positively about counselling and mental health services. Chrisna, aged 18 and from the DRC, said that her experience of counselling soon after she had come to the UK had helped her. While the process was painful, as indicated by other young people, she also felt it had been beneficial:

*I talked to her [the counsellor] about some of my personal things. I needed to talk to someone. She felt that I was kind of keeping everything inside and I showed that I had a lot in my mind. She told me that you have a lot on your mind, you must let it out, you must express it and you might feel better. It was both hurtful to let it out and helpful at the same time because I expressed. I had a lot in my mind, I had a lot in my heart and I let it out.*

Similarly Aliya, in response to being asked how she coped when she was feeling sad, said:

*Just crying, crying. I find it nice – I just let it out and I feel happier. I pray and then I just cry. I know that God is listening and won't judge me. I just have to express my thoughts, my feelings and I feel relief when I do that.*

She then went on to explain that she had received counselling for about six months after arriving in the UK and there she had been taught strategies to help her cope with her emotions:

*I will never forget. He [the counsellor] said, if you keep things in like, you know, where we keep the clothes – if we put wet clothes or dirty clothes in the drawer and don't take them out and wash them, then all the horrible things are going to stay there and smell. So we have to take out the bad thoughts, clean them, iron them and put them back.*

Maryam from Iran had reached a crisis in her mental health and attempted suicide. After this, she was allocated a support worker to work with her every day for a week. She said it helped her enormously to feel that she had someone to talk to, 'a friend' and this helped to build her confidence. On reflection, she felt that she would have benefited from more emotional support:

*Somehow, if they can let you know from the beginning how much emotional help you get from social services . . . For about five months I was completely lost and going through a really bad time and didn't have anyone to talk to. Now they are like my family to me, I actually enjoy going to see them at social services.*

Innocent from Nigeria had experienced several episodes of hospitalisation following attempts to take his own life. He also had clearly benefited from the weekly counselling sessions that he received:

*She [the counsellor] is helpful, she's really helpful. She is the one who said I shouldn't go back to Nigeria [under the voluntary repatriation programme]. The only person that I talk to is the counsellor – I can talk about the past. At that time [when he attempted suicide] I didn't . . . I would just cry a lot, drink too much. At first I said nothing to her and gradually I started talking to her.*

For those young people who described positive experiences of counselling services, it appeared to be the continuity of the counselling support over a period of time, combined with the opportunity to establish a trusting relationship with the professional providing the counselling, that made a difference to their lives. This finding seems to support the systematic review evidence for PTSD among adults indicating that single-session counselling has little or no effect (Rose *et al*, 2003).

---

### Implications for policy and practice

- There is a need to find ways of explaining the benefits of therapeutic mental health care to young people seeking asylum alone in the UK in a way which does not stigmatise or frighten them.
- Cultural understandings of mental health outside of the UK are often focused on severe mental illness, psychosis and "loss of control". The notion of services to support and promote mental health is not well understood by young people who arrive in the UK seeking asylum.
- There appears to be a real gap in terms of appropriate services that social care and health professionals can refer young people on to. CAMHS services across local authorities where young people are accommodated are reported to be over-subscribed and of very variable quality.
- There is a particular gap in appropriate services for young people once they reach the age of 18. In theory, they would then be referred into adult mental health services, but these are not configured in a way that can best support the specific needs of young people seeking asylum.
- A number of young people had specific concerns about what they perceived as inappropriate and over-use of medication to alleviate their emotional difficulties.
- There is evidence that some young people can benefit a great deal from the right therapeutic intervention.

---

- Counselling and therapeutic support may be better provided to some young people in less clinical settings, for example, as part of their care within a residential setting, provided that due attention is paid to issues of confidentiality and appropriate referral on to more specialist mental health services when required.
- There appears to be a general lack of appropriate training for primary care and other social care professionals to assist them in correctly identifying the more severe mental health difficulties that are sometimes experienced by young people seeking asylum.
- Although a few general practices are very experienced in working with asylum-seeking young people, there is a reported large variation in the quality of general practice and wide-spread lack of expertise and knowledge of the specific needs of asylum-seeking young people and how best to respond to these.
- Health professionals need to be aware of the impact on young people of worries about their immigration status (see Chapter 9), and to take into account the possibility that their stay in the UK may be temporary when planning the provision of therapeutic care.

# 7  Being in care

This chapter discusses the provision made by social care services for unaccompanied young people seeking asylum in the local authority hosting the research study. A key factor in young people's emotional well-being is their living situation, and the different kinds of placement used for young people in the study are considered in turn (formal and informal foster care, residential care, independent and semi-independent living). We then examine other aspects of young people's interaction with social care services that are likely to be relevant to their emotional well-being: their interaction with social workers, experience of age assessments and their entitlement to financial support.

Figure 3 shows the type of placement that young people were in at the time of our research. The "other" category refers to young people either living with family members (2), young people supported under section 4 of the Asylum and Immigration Act (1999), which was true for two young people, and a young person who had been formerly supported by the local authority but was recently dispersed at the age of 21 after having a baby.

*Figure 3*
**Type of placement at time of interview**

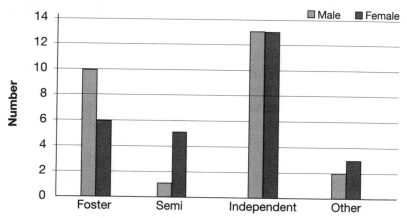

## Foster care

About 60 per cent of the young people who participated in the study had experienced – or were still experiencing – foster care since arriving in the UK. Of these, the vast majority were very positive about their time in a foster placement and about their relationship with their foster carer. For some, the foster carers had become their substitute family and provided the care and love they had lost after being separated from their own parents. Nadine, from Rwanda, described her first experience of being with a foster carer in England, at the age of 15, after her traumatic journey as a refugee:

*I found these lovely people . . . you know, it is just like a god-given family. I can't say they replaced my family but they were like there for me so much they become a family to me now. And you know they took care of me . . . she prepared a bath for me, everything, gave me new clothes . . . really lovely people. And they cooked for me and they said you can eat as much as you want . . . They made me feel so comfortable – they made me feel at home.*

Hellen, aged 17, from Ethiopia, was placed in foster care with Mahlet, also from Ethiopia, when she arrived at the age of 15. Hellen was full of praise for her foster carer, whom she likened to her 'mum':

*My foster mum was really nice, like my mum, she called us 'my daughters'. She trusted us for everything.*

Thierry, aged 16 and from Burundi, also likened his current carer to his 'mum' and said it was having the knowledge that she cared that had made all the difference to him. This was his second foster placement; the first one broke down partly because, he said, the carers wanted 'to know too much' and kept asking a lot of questions, which made him feel uncomfortable. He explained how his current foster placement (where he had lived for about two-and-a-half years) was so much better:

*It's nice, it's comfortable here. It just feels nice here, like my own house. They treat me like I am one of them, you know, not different. I know that my foster mum cares about me. Once I got arrested and when she came to bail me out, she was crying like she was my own mum. It made me think she's like my mum.*

The importance of support offered in a "good" foster placement, and the difference it could make to a young person's life, was also identified by many of the professionals we spoke to. As a specialist nurse for looked after children commented:

*I think if they're placed with foster carers, usually they have the support networks around them. So I think if you have foster carers that take on that day-to-day parental role, I think young people are a lot better off.*

The youngest of the unaccompanied children we spoke to appeared to be particularly well settled in foster care. Namir, an 11-year-old boy from Afghanistan, used to cry when he first went to the foster carer at the age of nine. The carer told us that she thought he was 'missing his mum. I used to hug him and say, "I'm your mum now".' Two years later, at the time of the study, Namir appeared to be a very happy, settled child. He described his placement like this:

*Mum [the foster carer] makes me happy. She is nice to me all the time. She cooks nice dinner, we go for walks. I go outside to play, I play on my bike and I play with some children in the block.*

Several of the young people, including Mahlet, Hellen and Nadine, were still in regular contact with their foster carer a long time after leaving the placement and went to see them frequently. Two of the young people we spoke to had foster carers who continued to care for them even after they had stopped being supported financially by the children's services department.

Living with carers or other children from the young person's country of origin was identified as being a very important factor in the success of the placement by many of the young people we spoke to. Zelgai, 11 years old and from Afghanistan, arrived in the UK when he was just nine and was placed with Lebanese carers and another Afghan boy:

*It is good here. There is another Afghan boy – he speaks the same language as me. So I talk to him; if I don't understand something, then I tell him to tell them.*

Another boy from Afghanistan, 15-year-old Asif, lived with a white British foster family for two years. Although he was quite happy there, he was concerned that he was losing his links with his culture, language and religion and was eventually moved to be with an Afghan family, where he could practise Islam and speak his first language. He explained the importance for him of living with a family from his own country:

*I get the chance not to forget my culture, I get the chance not to forget my religion, I get the chance not to forget my language.*

However, some of the young people we spoke to had been placed with foster carers from different cultures and religions. Despite the importance of matching in terms of language, culture and faith that has been identified as central to the success of foster placements (see, for example, Kidane, 2001; Hek, 2005a), most of these young people had had very positive experiences of cross-cultural placements. Ajani, for example, an 18-year-old young man from Afghanistan and a practising Hindu, had been placed with African carers and two other boys, one from Ethiopia and one from Eritrea. He had developed a very strong and close relationship with his carers and felt that they had had learned much from each other. He was still in touch with them on a regular basis after leaving the placement. Another example was Simeon, a Muslim from Somalia who had arrived in the UK at the age of 13, and was placed with a Christian Nigerian family. He described the foster placement as 'hard at first' as we 'kept our distance' but bit by bit they grew to know and understand each other. He described his foster mother as 'the greatest mother ever seen' and added:

*I owe her a lot – she was a mother figure for me. We had a connection although we were from different cultures and different religions. No one can break us. I love her very much.*

Although the majority of the young people we spoke to had valued their time in foster care, some also described negative aspects, although these are not unique to asylum-seeking children and young people (see, for example, Sinclair, 2005). One common theme was the feeling that the foster family, however hard they tried, was not their 'real' family and that this knowledge had often 'got in the way' of their relationship. Asif, who had arrived in the UK from Afghanistan when he was 10, was very happy with his Afghan foster carers. However, he also felt at times that he did not quite fit in:

> *There are times when I feel sad. When they [the foster family] have their family around and you don't, you act a bit different, talk a bit different, sit somewhere different, try to communicate in the family but, you know, it works out sometimes and sometimes it doesn't.*

This experience was echoed by a 17-year-old young woman from Eritrea, Malashu, who did not always feel she 'belonged' to the foster family:

> *They do try and treat us as part of the family but it's not always easy to feel part of the family sometimes – that's the problem. There are times when they go out as a family and they don't ask us. Sometimes I really don't mind but sometimes it's not nice and then sometimes they meet up as a family, they are a really big family, instead of being happy with them and stuff, I don't like to join in.*

One children's services team manager we spoke to acknowledged that, in some cases, young people found it difficult to settle into a foster family. This could be for various reasons: either because the young person had some of their own family living elsewhere in England (sometimes placed in separate accommodation due to age differences), or because the young person put up emotional barriers between themselves and the carers:

> *Some kids go into foster care and want to be part of the family; most children have family somewhere so some kids go into foster care but don't want to be part of the family.*

Living with carers who did not have their own children enabled some young people to feel more settled and to develop a closer relationship with their carers. For example, Azyeb, an 18-year-old young woman from

Eritrea, explained how, although she had been placed in foster care with her younger sister, the placement had broken down as a result of problems between the carer and her sister:

*Foster carers can't be like your mum and dad – they can't be, never. The foster carer had a little girl and she [my sister] used to see how she treated her and it can't be the same. So she used to feel, like, jealous. She used to cry a lot. And they didn't really get on.*

Azyeb went on to talk about the foster carer she and her sister moved on to, a placement that was much more successful, for the following reasons:

*Because this lady is young lady, she don't have children, only young. She's like us, she can talk about anything and stuff.*

A number of young people in foster care also told us that they did not publicise the fact that they were in foster care to the people they met. Ruth, aged 13 from Eritrea, revealed:

*My friends at school don't know about me living with a foster carer. They just think I live with my mum.*

Overall, it appeared that when a foster placement worked well for a child or young person, this type of care could make a crucial difference to her or his well-being. Many of the professionals, social workers in particular, also held this view. "Good" foster placements were characterised by many social care professionals as being places that offered emotional support, stability, love, affection, a mother and/or a father figure, boundaries and guidance. Above all, a successful foster placement was one where the foster carer showed an active interest in the young person's well-being. As one children's asylum worker commented:

*If the foster carers show an interest, they can make a big impact on how their lives go. The same child who is placed with different foster families will have totally different outcomes.*

Not all foster carers with whom children seeking asylum were placed met these criteria for promoting their mental health and emotional well-being.

Some social care professionals we spoke to described situations where the young person was not given any boundaries (such as specific bedtimes and household rules), or where the foster carers were not particularly interested in the young person and saw their role as providing bed and breakfast, rather than having a wider supportive and parenting role.

## Informal or private fostering

Of the 54 young people whom we spoke to, only three had experienced informal fostering arrangements after arriving in the UK. One of these was an 18-year-old young man from Uganda, Peter, who had come to Britain when he was 13. He described how he and his brother had been abandoned in a Ugandan church shortly after arriving in England and that a member of the congregation had accommodated them with financial support from the local children's services department. At first, the placement worked well because, as Peter explained, the woman was also from Uganda and that helped them to communicate and understand each other. However, social services decided to stop supporting the arrangement. The woman had tried to continue looking after Peter but found that money provided through Income Support and Child Benefit was just not enough to care for him. Eventually, children's services reversed their decision and she was able to carry on supporting Peter. The major difficulty came when Peter started living independently when he was 18. It transpired that for a long time he had been supported under section 17 rather than section 20 of the Children Act 1989, meaning that he was not eligible for leaving care support under the leaving care legislation. At the time of the study, he was receiving help from an advocacy project to make an official complaint to children's services, with the aim of reversing the decision so that he could start receiving support under the Leaving Care Act. The additional pressures of seeking advocacy support alongside dealing with his immigration status had caused Peter a great deal of stress. He had had to defer a place at university and might need to repeat his final year of school since he had had to miss so much school to deal with these other issues. As a result, his grades had not been as good as he had hoped.

Simeon, from Somalia, became homeless after being mistreated in a private fostering placement with relatives. He described the experience as 'hell' and said there was 'abuse, shouting' and that they (the family) treated him 'like a slave', eventually 'kicking him out'. Simeon said that he did not trust people as a result of this and, despite being only 13 years old, he slept in the park for a few weeks. He was then helped by a teacher, who persuaded him to go to the local social services department after which he was placed in foster care.

## Residential care

A small number (five) of the young people we spoke to had experienced residential care in two different London boroughs. On the whole, those who had been in residential care had valued their time there. What made the residential placement successful or not, however, was the quality of relationships between the young people and the staff. The role of the key worker or specific member of staff in helping a young person settle in and feel "at home" was a consistent theme. Houmam, a 16-year-old young man from Syria, described one specific person at the residential home who helped him, a woman he likened to his 'mum' and who had given him money at Christmas time.

One young woman, Chrisna from the DRC, was particularly full of praise for her residential placement. The staff there had made her feel so welcome that she felt they were like another family. She praised the staff and her key worker, in particular, for giving care and support like parents would:

*My key worker I could talk to about everything really. My key worker and some of the others – they always used to be there for me. They always used to come and talk to you and help you express your feelings. It was comfort really so it made me feel comfortable to talk to them about everything. I was feeling sad, I was feeling lonely that I was away from my family so they really helped.*

## Semi-independent living

The majority of the young people we spoke to for the study had lived for at least a short while, usually during the period soon after their arrival in England, in a semi-independent housing block in the local authority, used specifically for unaccompanied asylum-seeking young people. Many praised the accommodation there – 'the rooms were really beautiful and spacious' (Zemar) – and the opportunity the shared accommodation provided for making friends. The Chinese, Eritrean and Ethiopian young women we spoke to appeared to particularly benefit from supportive friendships they established from living together. However, some young people criticised the accommodation for being noisy and for monitoring young people too much, for instance, by using CCTV cameras. A small number of young people had not lived in the block themselves, but had formed negative perceptions of the place from talking to others who had been accommodated there.

When talking about important people who had offered support, a significant number of young people identified the key worker allocated to them while living in semi-independent accommodation as crucial to their well-being. Much of the support that these young people had received, and valued highly, was practical help such as sorting out financial issues, shopping to furnish their room, help with college assignments, and so on. In addition to this practical help, key workers could be an important source of emotional support. Peter, from Uganda, noted that:

> *It wasn't just the professional help but I was able to relate to the person as a friend. Conversations were on the same kind of level.*

There were evidently clear benefits from having a key worker to support young people. However, this role was limited and most young people we spoke to were allocated such a worker for only four hours a week. Several professionals working in health and voluntary agencies commented on the centrality of the support offered by key workers and how it was often far more practical and personalised than the type of support and guidance provided by a social worker. This said, the number of key workers and the time that they had to spend with young people was, in their opinion, too limited.

## Independent living

Young people in independent accommodation were, unsurprisingly, more likely to describe times when they felt isolated or lacked the support they needed. This was particularly the case when, on reaching 18 years, they had been moved to different accommodation that was often away from friends with whom they might have been living for a number of years. The quality of the independent accommodation that was observed by researchers varied enormously. In some cases, young people had access to shared spaces in the house where they could eat as well as cook together and a separate living space for relaxation and communal living. In other cases, they had very basic shared cooking amenities and described having to eat alone in their bedrooms since there was no communal space to eat.

Living independently meant either living in a shared house or in a self-contained flat or bedsit. Compared to placements which offered some in-built support, either from a foster carer or key worker, many of the young people who were living independently were finding the experience difficult. They described being placed, aged 18, in accommodation with people they did not know. Some recounted having no shared space to eat meals and often talked of cooking and eating alone – although this was more commonly reported among young men than young women. Some young people reported feeling unsafe or that others in the house were unfriendly towards them. Those who had come from foster placements frequently found the pressures of shopping, cooking and organising a household alongside attending college and studying stressful.

As a specialist nurse for LAC said:

> *Moving into independent housing, that's one of the most difficult things, you know – they have said it to me – because they have no support. I think semi-independent is slightly better because there's a key worker or someone there that will just show you the basics.*

Some of the young people living in shared accommodation complained that they had to share facilities, such as one lavatory and a kitchen, with as many as six others. Claude took a photo of the toilet, to show the researcher how he had to share it with six others and then complained that there was no eating area in the accommodation. This meant that they all had to eat in their rooms, which made their rooms smell and was not conducive to making friends. Mesaret, despite feeling lonely, did not want to share with other young people; she found it difficult to share a fridge with others, as she did not eat pork. In the words of one social worker:

> *You put five young people in a shared house and expect them to share a kitchen, bathroom and living room when they come from five different societies and cultures. Lots of problems arise and cause additional stress.*

Other young people lived in single accommodation – either a one-bed-room or a studio flat – and described feeling very isolated there. Some, especially those who had experienced detention, either in the UK or in their country of origin, found the small physical environment they had to live in suffocating and imprisoning. During the study, one young man, Mahamat from Chad, who had previously been detained in the UK, was offered a tiny studio flat which made him feel as if he had returned to his prison cell. Mesaret, from Ethiopia, had fled to the UK after being raped in prison in her home country. She lived in a small bedroom in a house-share and commented that she could not 'stay in a closed area'.

Chrisna, from the DRC, who had lived in a residential unit with key worker support followed by a semi-independent placement (again with a key worker), found living alone difficult:

> *I like being here, but I found it quite hard living here. Since I moved it's been hard though, in terms of being by myself, living by myself and trying to manage the money. It's been hard, actually.*

One GP we spoke to echoed this sense of isolation experienced by many young people living independently:

> *Some of them get very lonely at that stage because they're much more obviously on their own. Some of them have had very little chance to develop any kind of support network by that stage and a good few of them have said, 'Look, I'm just lonely.'*

## Last resort accommodation

Four young people we spoke to had either reached the end of their appeals process through the asylum system or were no longer eligible for accommodation or support from the local authority children's services department. These young people lived in particularly difficult circumstances which undoubtedly created high levels of anxiety and stress for them.

Rakeb from Eritrea had been moved with her two-year-old son eleven times by the Border and Immigration Agency (BIA). At the time of the research she was receiving support under section 4 of the Immigration and Asylum Act (1999) which meant that she was not eligible for any direct financial or housing support but was given accommodation and vouchers to live on. She had had to move again recently with only two bags, so she could not take her baby's potty with her. She expressed powerlessness in this process, commenting: 'They just move us. We don't have the right to say no or yes.' Betania, from Angola, also accommodated under section 4, lived in a hotel with other "failed asylum seekers" where she shared a room with two other women. Like Rakeb, she survived on vouchers and was not eligible for any direct financial support.

Daisy, from China, had arrived in the UK when she was just 16 years old. At the age of 21 she had recently been sent to live in a local authority very far from where she had been living, and far from the father of her nine-month-old baby. She was not told about having to move until the day before, and arrived in a new authority some 200 miles away, not knowing anybody.

## Young people's experiences of social workers

The relationships that young people reported forming with social workers also had a substantial impact on their emotional well-being. Many young people in the study reported very positive relationships with their social workers. Aliya, a young woman from Somalia, described how she could talk to her social worker when she felt sad. She said it was like 'having a shoulder to cry on' and she enjoyed going to the local children's services department office, where they made her feel 'at home' and 'welcome'. She told us how children's services had given them phone cards at

Christmas so that they could phone home, which she said 'was a nice thought'. Christiana, an 18-year-old from Nigeria, likened social services to her parents:

*I feel like social services are like your parents, aren't they? That you can reach out to. Because with friends you can only talk but with social services they are providing you with stuff or financial help, with education. So they have been very helpful really, they have been very helpful, like finding me this education.*

Christiana went on to explain how she also had a lot of emotional support from her social worker, finding it 'easy to talk to her and easy to approach'. Asif, aged 15 from Afghanistan, told us why his first social worker was also his 'best':

*She followed me through every little step. I didn't have to tell her what was coming up, I didn't have to tell her to do things for me. With her, she looked at me in the eyes and knew exactly what was up. She knew me very, very well.*

As has been discussed in earlier research (e.g. Kohli, 2005), sometimes young people spoke about not wanting to talk about their backgrounds and the problems they faced, but social workers kept asking them 'questions'. Hellen from Ethiopia explained how this felt:

*Sometimes they don't understand when you are sad. They keep asking you questions. It makes me angry, it makes me want to shout. It makes me remember all the bad things and they don't understand that. If they ask me questions, I will suffer for months.*

Mahlet, a 16-year-old girl from Ethiopia, had little faith in her social worker. This was largely because the social worker kept mixing her up with someone else and got important information about her completely wrong. Another young person, Mahamat, felt strongly that social workers needed more knowledge and understanding about the background situations of asylum-seeking young people. Aliya expressed concern that her social worker kept talking about his own children, which made her feel very sad about missing her own father. She also felt strongly that she would prefer to have a woman social worker, which, she said, would help her feel more 'comfortable'. Zemar complained about the red tape involved across local authority departments. He gave an example: 'Your social worker is your guardian but he can't talk directly to housing people.'

Malashu from Eritrea felt that social workers did too much paperwork in front of young people and that 'they are not there for you'. She had also experienced a social worker breaking her confidence: Malashu had asked the social worker not to tell the foster carer that she was going to go for counselling. Because the social worker did then go and tell the foster carer about the counselling appointment, Malashu felt that she could not trust anybody and ended up cancelling it.

Some young people felt that they were being treated differently by social services compared to other young people. Aliya, from Somalia, felt frustrated that she could not get a specialist computer she needed because she had dyslexia, despite being able to "prove" it as a psychologist had written a letter of support. The difference between the specialist computer and an ordinary one, she said, was only £50. She felt strongly that her 'real parents would do this . . . it's just a difference of £50'.

Some too spoke of how they felt they had been treated differently by social workers and social services departments from non-asylum seeking young people who had recently left care. This had left them feeling confused and hurt. Some young people made distinctions between *their* "cases" being held in an "asylum" team, whereas "leaving care teams" supported other young people. Mahamat, a young man from Chad, had been in the UK for four years but was still living in temporary accommodation. He was angry that other young care leavers had already been given permanent accommodation but he had not. Simeon told us he felt that unaccompanied asylum-seeking young people were 'nothing' compared to young people from leaving care teams and that he had to 'pay for more things'. The perception of a two-tier support system, with young people seeking asylum receiving less support than other looked after children, was also raised by several professionals who were interviewed for this study. Several of them talked specifically about how the *Every Child Matters* agenda had failed to address the well-being needs of asylum-seeking children and young people.

A key theme in the interviews with young people was how variable the social work support had appeared to them. Many young people had experienced several changes of social worker and had found that they received very different information and levels of support. Nanu, from Eritrea, for example, had asked for money from social services towards books for college. At first, she could not get any money but then another social worker said that she would be able to just by producing the receipt, which she did. Consequently, many young people felt confused by the inconsistencies and mixed messages from different social workers and different social work teams.

## Age assessments

Several of the young people we spoke to had had their age disputed by social services, sometimes a year or so after they had arrived. These age assessments and disputes had caused them considerable anxiety as well as anger and frustration that they were not being believed. The actual process of conducting age disputes was perceived as degrading and intrusive. Ibrahim, aged 19 and from Pakistan, was 16 when he entered the UK. After many months of uncertainty about whether or not the social services department would continue to support him, since they claimed he was not the age he said he was, his solicitor sent him for an independent age assessment from a doctor. He explained:

*The doctor see my teeth, he checked my skin and everything and he said that my age was correct and I have the medical report now.*

It was particularly difficult for young people when their age was disputed years after arriving in the UK. In these cases, the disputes had resulted in major changes in the young people's lives, in that they had to move from foster care or school or meant that they had to "grow up" more quickly. Kiki, from Eritrea, came to the UK when she was 15 but because her age was disputed, with social services saying she was between 17 or 18 years of age, she never lived in foster care and instead had to live independently in a guest house. Another young person, Patrick from the DRC, arrived in the UK when he was 12. He was placed in foster care but the placement broke down. After a dispute with the foster carer and getting into trouble at school, he was subjected to an age assessment by social services. This had the result that at the age of 15 (according to Patrick) he was having to live on £44 per week with a friend of his sister's, a very insecure arrangement. He very much saw the age assessment and dispute at the time as a punishment for getting into trouble at school.

Chrisna, who arrived from the DRC at the age of 15, had her age assessed and disputed by social services and found the whole experience very traumatic. She described the process, which revealed discrepancies between physical characteristics and emotional maturity:

> It [the age assessment] was such a horrible experience. My social worker did it. They checked my teeth, skin, my height and everything. The doctor said I was between 19 and 21 but I was only 16. But the people in the children's home agreed I was 16 because they were living with me every day; they could see my behaviour and how I was with the other young people.

Chrisna said that the assessment from the residential unit helped her case because after that the social services manager stopped disputing her age. However, the relationship Chrisna had with her social worker, who had instigated the process, had been irreparably damaged by the process:

> It was hard. It was hard because she was against me, she was really against me. I liked her but I felt she didn't like me. After that she told me I had to have another worker as she couldn't work with me any more . . . things like that.

Some of the social care professionals we spoke to also expressed concern about the age assessment process. As one social services team manager explained, many young people who have their age assessed upon arrival in the UK have been travelling for days, weeks and sometimes months or even years. They are emotionally and physically exhausted, with the result that they can often look much older than they actually are. As she said:

> Two days later, when they have some decent food and some good sleep, you can see the freshness of their youth again.

Another social worker felt strongly that the age assessment process was the most problematic area of social work practice with unaccompanied children and young people:

> *We do them [age assessments] but we can be wrong five years either side – it matters a lot, doesn't it? They can end up with many dates of birth – social services, Home Office, their own – they get muddled up. They don't always understand why we do it, what difference it makes. We explain why but the process is not always clear. At every stage it's a problem.*

Another professional, a children's rights officer working with asylum-seeking young people, also identified age assessments as a very difficult area which often left young people feeling angry and confused. One young man she had worked with had had his age assessed and disputed, and she subsequently saw his mental health deteriorate, partly because the dispute had forced him to leave his educational placement.

One of the reasons for the age disputes appears to be linked to the cultural differences between childhood in the UK and in other countries, and the expectations that are attached to how a young person of a certain age should or should not behave. In many cases, too, the young people we spoke to had had to grow up more quickly because of their experiences of trauma, loss, war and abuse. Joy, a 17-year-old from Nigeria who arrived in the UK when she was 13, explained how her foster care placement broke down and that her age was subsequently disputed. This was partly because, she said, the foster carer felt she was not behaving as a child should:

> *That woman where I was staying [foster carer] she was having problem with me 'cos she said I was not jumping around with those children and I was meant to be jumping around with them. And I told her that it is not me, because I am actually a child but at the same time an adult, you know.*

Many professionals we spoke to also commented on the problems that could arise from expecting a young person's allocated social worker to conduct an age assessment. At the time of writing (as briefly discussed in

Chapter 1) the Government was considering alternative arrangements for age assessments and relevant research (Crawley, 2007) had recommended that age assessments be conducted through independent regional age assessment centres.

## Finances and entitlements

When young people reach 18 years of age, their financial allowances are substantially reduced and most of them have to cope on very limited resources – about £40 a week. While in foster care and before they are 18 they are entitled to clothing allowances, free travel and other financial support, but once 18 they are likely to receive social and housing benefits rather than direct resources from the local authority. Azyeb, who was 18 at the time of the research and had arrived from Eritrea when she was 12, reflected that the allocation of resources which involved giving younger children much more money than those who were older, seemed to be inappropriate. She explained:

> *They shouldn't give you a lot of money when you're little . . . they make you used to the money and then they cut it down so you feel like, what's going on? It's like a rich person going poor. I think they should change that and give you little money when you are younger and then more money as you get older . . . to keep yourself.*

Despite the fact that there is some guidance available which clarifies the rights and entitlements of unaccompanied children and young people (see, for example, Save the Children, 2005), there was no doubt that young people were extremely confused about what they were and were not entitled to in terms of continuing financial support and wider benefits, and that this was particularly the case once they reached 18 years. Many young people over 18 said that they struggled on the £45 they were given. Some who were still in education received an educational maintenance allowance (EMA) that enabled them to manage during term time, but struggled during holidays when they did not receive the EMA and their income was substantially reduced.

Chrisna described how hard it was to cope on limited finances:

*If you have £45–50 a week and you have to think of eating, you have to think of clothing, you have to think of washing liquid, toiletries, things for college . . . it's nothing.*

Having to pay for their own travel to and from college once they were 18 years old was a significant drain on young people's limited resources. Others described how they would really like to join leisure centres and sports facilities, but simply did not have the money.

For those young people supported under section 4 of the Asylum and Immigration Act (1999), such as Rakeb, all benefits were provided in vouchers and they had no access to cash. Rakeb, now aged 21, found this particularly difficult with her young son. She commented on how she couldn't even take her son for a ride in the toy cars outside the super-market because she had no coins or money.

For some young people, just the process of going to collect their money each week or each fortnight was something they dreaded and found degrading. In the words of Mahlet:

*I feel like I am just begging for money. I have to take the money 'cos I can't live without buying things and food – but I don't like it.*

When asked about whether she would continue to have financial support and assistance throughout her university course, Maryam commented:

*I don't know how it works but they [social services] said they don't give it to anyone.*

Nanu, a 20 year-old young woman with a four-year-old child, described how she was given conflicting information by different workers in the social services department and at the job centre, and had to enter complex negotiations with staff at the job centre before they would allow her to continue to access her benefits and stay on in full-time education.

Whether or not young people were entitled to go to university and whether they could access courses without having indefinite leave to remain was another area of confusion for them. Mahlet from Ethiopia, for example, said she wished universities could be more flexible – even if she was granted a further three years to remain and then was sent home, she knows that she could complete her degree in nursing before then and did not understand why she should not be allowed to do this.

---

## Implications for policy and practice

- Foster placements when they work well can provide essential support to asylum-seeking young people, who are usually placed with foster carers when below the age of 16 years. However, it is the quality of the relationship between the carers and the young person that is the most vital element of this support.
- Placements that can maintain a link with language and culture are important, but such matching is not always crucial; this will depend on the young person and the carers. The individual needs and wishes of young people need to be taken into account.
- For asylum-seeking young people not in foster placements, there is clear value in them having access to a one-to-one key worker or mentor who can provide personalised and comprehensive support.
- Young people who experienced residential care provided specifically for children seeking asylum, were very positive about the support they received and the quality of the relationships they established with staff within the home.
- The expectation that allocated social workers should conduct age assessments of young people is problematic. This risks undermining any trusting relationship that a professional might have built with a young person up to that point. Our study would support other research that has recommended that age assessments be conducted by independent regional centres.
- Social workers and other professionals need to understand different experiences of childhood in different cultures. Many unaccompanied asylum-seeking young people have had to mature more quickly as a result of traumatic and abusive experiences, or as a result of assuming many adult responsibilities from an early age.

- Young people participating in the study reported a lack of consistency, fairness and equity in how social care support, including financial, educational and social work support, is provided to asylum-seeking young people.
- Staff in the different agencies who are likely to come into contact with young people seeking asylum often lack sufficient information and knowledge in terms of eligibility for housing and social benefits and other services. This implies the need for joint training and guidance between relevant agencies.
- There is an evident need for clear and accessible information for asylum-seeking young people about their eligibility for support and how they can best access this.

# 8 The impact of education

Attending school or college, while it may be challenging especially for those asylum-seeking children and young people who speak little English on arrival, has been shown to provide an important "normalising" experience which contributes to their emotional well-being (Candappa and Egharevba, 2000; Rutter, 2003; Hek, 2005b). In this chapter we discuss the types of educational experiences that young people reported having in the UK and how these affected their state of mind.

## The wider benefits of learning

Most young people interviewed valued highly the educational opportunities they had received after arriving in the UK. Their previous educational experiences were very variable. Some came from situations where war and conflict had meant they had never been to school, or had had limited primary or elementary education. Others had had sporadic access to education, sometimes in makeshift classrooms in private houses or in refugee camps. However, others came from highly educated backgrounds with parents who were in the top echelons of civil service or government in their countries. These young people had frequently had access to private education, which also often meant that they had developed their English language skills, thus making the transition and integration into the English education system easier.

In terms of emotional well-being, education most commonly was described as a means of distraction and a way of keeping busy. Similar to findings in other research, many of the young asylum seekers who participated in our study derived a great deal of enjoyment from school and identified it as one of the key things that helped them to feel well and happy. A number of young people described spending extensive amounts of time outside school hours on the school premises – either studying in the library or taking part in extra-curricular activities. Malashu, aged 17 from Eritrea, found that:

*When I make myself concentrate on studies, then I kind of forget everything. That's why I like learning because it makes me think of the future and forget the past.*

Mahlet from Ethiopia said:

*College makes me feel better 'cos I don't feel anything when I am in college. I just keep myself busy and then I come home and sit by myself and I think a lot of things.*

School featured as a place of safety and comfort in many of the accounts, particularly of the younger children we spoke to. Thirteen-year-old Zalmai, who had arrived from Afghanistan at the age of 11, talked very positively about the social experiences he had at school:

*There are no bullies there. I have loads of friends and they all have good behaviour. I have friends from many different countries – some are Arabic, Pakistani, Somali, British and Russian. We all play together and sometimes go swimming.*

Zemar, who arrived aged 16 from Afghanistan and was now 20, commented:

*College was like a haven for me you know, a safe haven where I could go and hide. I'd be in the college morning to evening every day.*

Namir, aged 11, talked of how he had a wide mix of American, Iranian, English and Jamaican friends. The local authority in which our study was located and the other London boroughs where some children were placed in foster care all had ethnically mixed populations and this multicultural environment appeared beneficial for young people in terms of their adaptation and integration. Malashu, now aged 17 and who had arrived at 15 from Eritrea, said:

*One of the things that I liked is that everyone kind of accepted me and didn't ask many questions. They made me feel happy. At school there were different people, different cultures and different religions.*

This finding is important when considered in relation to government plans to manage the arrangements for unaccompanied asylum-seeking children in the near future, as outlined in *Better Outcomes: The way forward* (Border and Immigration Agency, 2008). This includes dispersing unaccompanied children and young people to local authorities outside of the South-East region. It will be key to ensure that there is a level of cultural diversity in these areas since this appears to be very important to enhancing young people's sense of belonging and identity.

Many young people described teachers and tutors as 'very kind', 'lovely', 'helpful', and the atmosphere in the college and school as positive and warm. Thierry, from Burundi, said of the teachers at his secondary school:

*The teachers . . . they show you everything. If I ask for water, that's just an example, I get water. I don't get Pepsi if I ask them for water, that's why the teachers are helpful. If I ask them for this, they give me what I've asked for.*

William from the DRC commented about the individualised support that was so important to him:

*They [tutors] are nice, they are really nice . . . There is one thing that I have found between African and white . . . like, you know, like, they take someone else's place to help him and to learn him to catch up and to get what he wants without getting anything from the guy – you know what I mean?*

Many of the young people to whom we spoke had very high educational aspirations, wanted to progress from school or college to university and to make something of their lives. Nursing, pharmacy, medicine and law were common areas of careers and interests. Those who were less academic tended to focus on vocational studies such as catering and construction work.

Fifteen-year-old Ali, who arrived from Afghanistan at the age of 13, highlighted education as one of the things that made him feel happy. He had high aspirations and was completing his GCSEs at the time of the research. He then hoped to go into the sixth form and study science and maths, with a view to studying medicine at university:

*You want to become something in your life – you don't want your life to be, like, meaningless. That's why you have to get your education, to become something.*

Education was also seen as the means of 'making a better life' and doing well. A number of young people were quite candid about the combined reasons that they had been sent to the UK – to secure their safety while at the same time affording them a better education or chance of a 'better life'. Malashu, aged 17, described how she thought that the college she was attending was far better than her last school because 'I love learning and I have high aspirations.' Her current college had a very good reputation. She was studying for five "A" levels as well as Arabic and Italian as extra subjects. Her aim was to complete a politics degree, work for the United Nations and 'help make the world a better place'.

The benefits of a UK education for some young people were quite striking. Aliya's only access to education in Somalia had been the Madrassa (religious school) between the ages of 10 and 13. Being a Muslim, she was always struck by how difficult she had found it to learn Arabic and follow the Koran, and had always considered herself to be not very intelligent. Soon after her arrival in the UK, Aliya was diagnosed as having dyslexia and was given specialist support at college. As a result she had done extremely well at college, was planning to study nursing at university and described how her confidence had grown beyond recognition.

Frequently, young people identified a single tutor or teacher who had provided them with support beyond their educational needs. The social benefits of education and being part of an educational establishment, whether school or college, were also described positively by young people. As reported on later, friendships were central to their sense of well-being and were often their main source of emotional as well as practical support. Malashu particularly liked the fact that at her college young people could wear what they liked. This, she felt, opened her eyes to how many different people there were – 'punks', 'gothic people'.

Fifteen-year-old Asif had arrived from Afghanistan when he was 10 years old. He felt that because he had been in the UK for a relatively long time, he was very well known locally and had lots of different friends. He said that he was very popular with everyone and this was because he was friendly. The fact that the school was very "mixed" culturally had also really helped him to make many friends.

For younger children especially, school provided access to sports facilities which they enjoyed greatly. Playing sport was seen as a way to make new friends, as well as a welcome distraction and an important norm-alising activity. Eleven-year-old Zelgai, who arrived from Afghanistan at the age of nine, talked of how he played football, hockey and did running at school. Namir, aged 11 and from Afghanistan, loved playing cricket and, according to his foster carer, was very good at it. Fifteen-year-old Hossain, who arrived from Afghanistan aged 12, had been introduced to rugby since arriving in the UK and now played both rugby and cricket for the school team. He commented, 'I like being active in doing something.'

For those who were thriving in education, it appeared to be a combination of the support they were receiving and their own deter-mination to do well that led to their success. Nadine had arrived in the UK at the age of 15, completed nine GCSEs in a single academic year ('I used to stay after school, like up to 7.30 in the evening, and do my coursework'), successfully completed four "AS" levels and then three "A" levels with high grades. At the time of the research, she was completing her first year of a Psychology degree at university. Nanu had arrived from Eritrea aged 16 and six months pregnant after having been raped by soldiers in Eritrea. She organised access to childcare provision herself through Care2Learn (the social worker had not known about this service), completed an ESOL class in one year and at the time of her participation in the research was about to complete a three-year BTEC course in computing. Her son was by now four years old and she was applying to go to university to complete a degree in computer studies. Betania from Angola had never been accepted as eligible for support from the social services department, since her age was disputed when she arrived. As a result she was financing her own Access to Nursing course at a local college by working illegally and borrowing money. She was receiving limited support under section 4 of the Immigration and Asylum Act (1999) in the form of vouchers and had to share a room in a hostel with two other women. In order to find some quiet space to study, she had to use the kitchen after everyone in the large hostel had finished cooking.

## Barriers to education

Despite their determination and the success they had achieved, many young people seeking asylum faced difficulties in moving on further with their education. The older they were on arrival in the UK, the more difficult it was for them to access and benefit from education. On a practical level, arriving part-way through a school year could pose difficulties in gaining a place at a local school. Some young people described long periods when they had to wait for an opportunity to enter school or college. Saba, for example, aged 14 when she took part in the study, arrived from Eritrea when she was only 12. It took more than six months for her to be allocated a place at a local secondary school.

Those who had completed their secondary education faced further challenges as they attempted to move into higher education. Nadine, for example, described how she had faced many obstacles getting the support that she required. Accessing a student loan had been particularly difficult for her and meant that she had had to turn down two places at her chosen universities before the local authority agreed at the last minute to give her a loan and she was only able to secure a university place through the clearing house. These and other experiences left Nadine feeling that she would always be treated slightly differently to other people. For instance, while her friends at college planned a trip to France during the holiday, she was unable to go with them since she had no passport. It was these subtle differences that got her down at times. She explained:

*Sometimes I feel like I am fitting and then there is just that thing that happens and it kind of reminds you that you will always be singled out . . . Till that really important document [indefinite leave to remain] comes.*

Similarly, although Nanu had a place at university, she currently had no chance of securing a student loan since her application with the Home Office was pending and technically she had no status in the UK. Faced with the prospect of having to pay her own fees of £3,000 a year and knowing that this was not feasible, she felt it was more likely that she would have to settle for an HND course at the local college. At least two young people who participated in the study were paying their own tuition fees at university, despite having been looked after by local authorities and being in full-time education. Samuel, now 23, had arrived from Eritrea when he was 16 years old. After being refused a student loan to study information systems, Samuel borrowed money from friends and secured some support from local charities to finance his studies.

Despite doing well at school or college, young people frequently questioned the point of studying so hard. Maryam, now 21 years old and having arrived in the UK at 17, described how she found it increasingly difficult to concentrate on education when she felt so unsure about the future:

> *It's really stressful. I ask, 'What I am doing this for?' Two months before I graduate, they might ask me to leave the country. You just don't know; it's really horrible. You tell yourself to try and build up your life but then it all comes back, you can't ignore it all the time. There are two different sides of your life – on the one side you are trying to build it up and find wide experiences and do this and do that so your CV will look good and get a job and build up your future and on the other side, you don't know if you'll be able to live here the day after tomorrow. So why are you doing all these things?*

Mahlet similarly said:

> *Sometimes I just lose all my hopes and think, 'So why am I studying?' My father, I don't know where he is [taken away by the authorities], my mother is dead, my brother is dead, I am by myself, why I am studying? I am just keeping myself busy to not, like, bother.*

There were also other situations where educational experiences created anxieties and stress for young people. As already mentioned, some experienced having to wait for long periods of time before actually being able to attend school. Others talked about problems arising from inappropriate educational assessments when they entered a school. Not having earlier educational experiences taken into account and assumptions made about how well young people could do solely based on their language ability, resulted in a number being placed in a foundation level stream when they felt capable of achieving and working at a far higher level. The effects of this could be either a decrease in motivation or a loss of valuable time working their way up through the various ability levels in the school before they were able to achieve their full potential. Miguel, for example, arrived from Angola at the age of 12. He was placed at a foundation level for all subjects when he knew that he was capable of working at a far higher level. He says he was de-motivated and did not work hard and that his frustration combined with the difficulties he was facing with his home and social life. As a result, he failed his GCSEs. By contrast, his experience of college since leaving school had been very positive and he felt that far more attention had been paid at college to his personal learning needs. At the time of the research, at 18, Miguel had successfully re-taken his GCSEs and was completing his "A" levels. He planned to go on to study bio-sciences at university.

When Kenneh arrived from Liberia aged 13 years old, he was placed in a school where he says there 'were no white children, just foreigners'. He was then expected to attend English classes when he could already speak English quite well. He described getting bored and as a result dropped out of school. Requests to move to another school were not followed up by his social worker. Kenneh had had no formal education until he began a BTEC course in business studies when he was 16 years old.

Seventeen-year-old Malashu talked of how she never told other people that she was an asylum seeker because when she was at school she felt that some teachers treated her differently to others. They were 'nicer' to her and 'showed pity'. She also felt that they made assumptions that English would be difficult for her when in fact it was not.

Other young people emphasised how their ability to get on well in education was inextricably linked to how well they felt settled, and whether they had adequate and appropriate accommodation and access to resources and support. Maryam from Iran described how difficult she found it trying to study in a house with three other young women from another country, who did not have the same interests or priorities as herself. She had to put up with loud music every day, other people coming to the house and fighting – the police were often involved. When she tried to ask them to be quieter, they began to taunt and tease her. Maryam became so unhappy and, in her own words, 'depressed' that she attempted suicide and ended up in hospital. It was only after this event, despite repeatedly being asked to move, that the other girls were moved from the house and two others moved in with whom she got on well.

More generally, social care practitioners felt there was a lack of communication between the staff at colleges attended by young people seeking asylum and themselves. Although they might be told if a young person was failing to attend lessons on a regular basis, there was little other communication about their general well-being. Other professionals also felt that better communication between education and other services would increase understanding among professionals about the other aspects of young people's lives. One example given was that young people often had appointments, such as medical or legal, and yet the colleges frequently insisted on a hundred per cent attendance.

The current immigration system for children and young people means that they are in effect restricted in terms of their access to education – and their immigration status largely dictates what educational opportunities they can and cannot access. There was an evident lack of clarity and understanding among young people about how their immigration status affected their eligibility to educational access and resources and a clear need to find ways of explaining these entitlements to young people.

---

**Implications for policy and practice**

- The social, educational and wider benefits of education for children and young people seeking asylum are potentially extensive. Placing children and young people in quality, appropriate and well-supported educational placements as early as possible is central to their sense of well-being.
- Appropriate assessment of individual learning abilities and needs, which includes a verbal account of achievements and educational experiences prior to coming to the UK, would ensure that young people are able to work to their full potential from the earliest opportunity.
- Concerns and anxieties about other aspects of their lives, such as accommodation placements, their immigration status or

---

other issues, can negatively impact on young people's ability to fully benefit from a learning environment. The provision of holistic mentoring support for young people to help them cope with these wider concerns would also benefit their education.

- Opportunities to strengthen communication between education and social care professionals may help support young people better during difficult times of transition in their home or school lives.

- There is a distinct lack of guidance and support in terms of eligibility for financial and other support for those young people who want to progress to university. There was a perceived lack of consistency and equity in terms of how the decisions governing access to student loans are made and confusion in terms of eligibility for student loans for asylum-seeking young people who are eligible for support under the Children (Leaving Care) Act (2000).

# 9   Experiences of immigration and legal services

## Immigration status

Their immigration status in the UK was undoubtedly the area of greatest concern for young people we spoke to, particularly those who were aged over 16 and were supported by the youth asylum team or the transition team. Sometimes, when the issue of immigration status arose in the course of the research, young people showed visible distress – their faces would change or body language would indicate that it was upsetting for them to discuss this issue. At the time of the fieldwork, only four young people participating in the study had received indefinite leave to remain in the UK. The remainder were at various stages in their applications to stay.

It became apparent as the research progressed that for most of the young people in the study (except the younger ones who were in foster care), immigration status and the possibilities for the future regarding their status was the central issue that dominated their more immediate anxieties, concerns and fears. They often described the turmoil of turning ideas around in their heads and asking questions: What if they send me back? Where will I go? What will I do? Will they come looking for me? Will I be killed? Will I survive? Frequently, just talking about their immigration status to the researchers made young people very emotional. Faith, from Nigeria, became overwhelmed as she said:

> *I'm afraid, my papers are nearly finished. Before they gave me two years but it finishes in June – I don't want to go back to my country. I think about it every day.*

For those young people who faced severe depression and anxieties, the uncertainty regarding their status in the UK was at times unbearable. Rakeb clearly expressed how her depression, which she referred to as her 'darkness', was exacerbated by her uncertain future:

*Most of the time it feels darker than other days. I just want to go to the light, make myself happy. I am fighting too much to make my baby and myself happy – I am fighting every day. The feelings just come in front of me killing all the feelings of being happy. But the status thing gets in the way, affects everything. I feel like it is a big mountain in front of me and I can't shift it . . . it stops me from being myself.*

Similarly, Ibrahim, who had at the time of the research reached the end of the appeals process and feared imminent repatriation, said:

*I can't sleep here because no college, no nothing. Only sleep here . . . I can't do anything, I'm not allowed to work. I'm not allowed to do anything, you know, because three years have finished and I am still here [Ibrahim breaks down crying at this point]. And I go to doctor and he gives me tablets and I have depression. The Home Office, they don't listen. I went to the Home Office because I was crazy and mad, you know, and I said, 'You know my problems.' I said I don't under-stand. I said I have been coming here every month for three years . . . This is not freedom, it's like I'm in jail.*

The association between immigration status and emotional well-being was also frequently mentioned by professionals working with asylum-seeking young people:

*There's a lot of emphasis on the current asylum process and when that's uncertain that shakes up everything, I think. It can also be a sense of focus.* (Social work team manager)

*At age 17– 18, when they know their status is up for review, they start panicking. There is then an increase of mental health issues across the board, across all nationalities.* (Manager of residential unit for unaccompanied young people seeking asylum)

Many young people participating in the study had reached the end of their discretionary leave to remain and had made an application to have their leave extended so they could stay in the UK. This application had to be made before they reached their 18th birthday. Many said they had had no confirmation that their application had been received. Others had received letters confirming their application for further leave. The most common response from the Home Office was that, given the backlog of some 500,000 pending applications for asylum, it could be up to five years before a decision could be made about their asylum application. The standard letter said that, during that time, they could sustain the same rights to education and employment they had for the duration of their discretionary leave.

Mahlet was aware of the exact date when her leave would expire. She was extremely anxious about a possible interview with the Home Office. The basis of her claim was the persecution and death of her mother and possibly her father for their affiliation to a particular political party. Mahlet was worried that the information she would tell the hearing about the party would be out of date and that this would weaken her claim to asylum.

There was clearly a confusion about what young people were and were not entitled to do in terms of work, study and their eligibility for support while their application with the Home Office was still pending. Those who had received a letter from the Home Office indicating up to a five-year wait for their application to be resolved did normally have written confirmation of their eligibility to work. Others who were still waiting for a response were technically in limbo in terms of their eligibility to work and study.

Even when the Home Office allowed them to work, potential employers would often refuse to employ anybody who did not have a passport. Mireille was 18 years old and had arrived from Cameroon when she was 16. She had a young baby and was studying part-time for a BTEC qualification in business studies. She wanted to secure a part-time job to help with her finances but explained:

*I am allowed to work but some companies are cautious about it as I don't have a passport.*

Similarly, Nadine knew that she interviewed very well for all the part-time jobs she had applied for, but when potential employers saw that she did not have a passport, their reactions changed:

*They say you are really good . . . everything, but once they come to get that passport form . . . everybody is taking out their passport. And once I call them aside and say, 'Can I have a word with you?' and once they see those [immigration] papers they are not going to get back to me at all – and I have noticed that. And I have just learned to live with it. I go there and they look really confident and they even tell me you, you know, there is no reason for us not to give you [the job]. We will get back to you. But once they don't get back to you, I just know it's because of that paper. And it's just put everything on hold so much that sometimes it just hurts.*

Many young people described how they felt treated differently because of their status as an asylum seeker. Watching friends from college make their applications for student loans while they were not eligible, difficulties in opening a bank account, not being able to travel, problems in finding part-time work were all indicative to them that they were treated differently and had less status in this country than other young people.

Sebel from Ethiopia commented:

*You can't plan anything. You know if I want a driving licence or anything – they are just asking for passport and everything. You can't move . . . you can't plan anything . . . because everything they are just asking for your status – for me it's a big thing in my life . . .*

Young people in foster placements indicated much lower levels of anxiety surrounding their immigration status. This was due to a number of reasons. Firstly, those placed in foster care were younger and so did not have to worry about their status for several years. Even under the New Asylum Model, where discretionary leave may only be granted up to 17½ years, young people in foster placements often had a number of years left where they could concentrate on settling in the UK. Ruth, for example, had arrived aged 12 and was granted five years discretionary leave. Interviewed at the age of 13, she still had a further four years before her immigration status became a major concern for her and commented, 'I don't worry about it.'

Yemi, who was 16 and from Nigeria, said that although she thought about her immigration status sometimes, it was important to put it out of her mind because she had no control over it: 'There's nothing I can do, so I have to wait and see.'

Those young people who were nearing 18 years, or who were 18 and over and still had an application pending with the Home Office about their leave to remain in the UK, were constantly worried about it. Several of them likened the situation to being in "prison", reflecting their feelings of being in limbo and having no status, no citizenship, not being able to work, sometimes unable to study, unable to travel.

However, some older young people seemed to be able to focus on other aspects of their lives without their immigration status getting in the way. Kenneh talked of how it was better for him not to pay attention to the 'asylum thing' because otherwise he would just 'get stuck'. He said:

*It's important to me but it's not something I should be thinking about every day because if I think about that, then I have to think about my family, my country, I have to think about what happened. To me, I have to think about a lot of things 'cos . . . I want to leave the past behind. I want to forget it. I'm not changing my culture, yeah, but I'm living here now, innit, and I have to be like other young people here. That's it. Whatever happens, happens. If it's meant to happen, it happens, that's all I can say.*

For the few young people who had reached the end of their appeals process and were categorised under section 4 of the Immigration and Asylum Act (1999), the limitations on their freedom were greater. They had to report to the Home Office every two weeks, had no cash allowance but were only eligible to receive vouchers for food and clothing, and had no eligibility for housing, work, study or travel.

Rakeb, who had a two-and-a-half-year-old child at the time of the research, commented:

*I am not entitled to get housing, I'm not entitled to work, I'm not entitled to get anything in this country and I can't travel to find out about my family – I can't do anything . . . I can't support myself, I can't support my child . . . I feel like I've come from that small prison back home to prison in England.*

101

Alban, now 20 and having been in the UK for five years, had reached the end of his appeals process and had been detained in preparation for deportation back to Albania. He described having severe panic attacks within his cell and was very unwell. Eventually, with support from his foster carer, his school and his local MP and the intervention of the High Court, Alban was allowed to remain in the UK for a further three years.

Only two young people in the study had applied for voluntary repatriation to their countries and both felt that they had done so out of desperation. Importantly, both had experienced and continued to experience severe mental health difficulties and were still receiving psychiatric support. Mental health professionals working with both young people had advised them to withdraw their applications for voluntary return because they were not well enough to go, and because they would have very limited access to medical support once they left the UK.

Now that he is 19 years old, Ibrahim has been asked to report every month to the Home Office – an indication, he knows, that he might be deported at any time:

> *Every month I am going there and last time I asked, 'Please help me about this,' you know, 'Can you give me information about how long I have to come more?' you know . . . I am coming three years every month.*

## Returning "home": identity and belonging

Closely linked to their status here in the UK were the wider questions for young people relating to their identity and belonging. For many, confusion about this issue began before they left their homes.

Young people from Eritrea, and to a certain extent Ethiopia, faced particular turmoil with regard to their identity. Many described never having made the distinction between being Ethiopian and being Eritrean prior to the relatively recent conflict during which the Ethiopian government decided to expel all Eritrean people from Ethiopia. Many of the young people arriving in the UK had dual parentage – having one parent who was Eritrean and one who was Ethiopian. They had experienced expulsions to Eritrea where they did not speak the language and had often never set foot in the country before they were forced to go there. They also described feeling unwelcome in Eritrea since they were considered no longer to belong there – having spent all their lives in Ethiopia. Several discussions with young people from Eritrea and Ethiopia centred around the confusion this caused for them. If they were returned, where would they go back to?

Samuel, for example, had come from Ethiopia but was born to Eritrean parents. He had always thought of himself as Ethiopian because he lived there but now felt differently:

> *. . . since the government has denied what we are . . . so I decide not to be Ethiopian. Because of them I am suffering because I am Eritrean [i.e. born to Eritrean parents].*

He described how he had been to the Ethiopian embassy and they had refused to grant him documents as an Ethiopian citizen. Nanu talked about the prospect of returning to Ethiopia or Eritrea and felt that she could not go to either place – Ethiopia because she had seen how people turned against the Eritrean people – nor Eritrea where she had been subjected to such trauma.

Not surprisingly, during the course of the research we came across many close friendships between girls who were from Eritrea and Ethiopia. They were often placed together in shared housing and spent most of their free time together in mixed groups, i.e. from both countries. The distinction between the two countries was described as unreal for them.

For young people who had made complex journeys over many years before arriving in the UK, defining a sense of belonging was difficult. They had often assimilated many different languages and felt so far removed from their culture of birth that it would be like starting all over again if they were returned. The overwhelming majority of study participants wanted to remain in England, at least for the foreseeable future, rather than return to their countries of origin or move to another country.

Others felt that the length of time they had spent in the UK had changed them. William expressed this well:

> *I am just thinking, if I go back how life is going to be like. I am just somebody different than what I was before, you know. I don't know*

*how it is going to be like . . . it's strange, strange. It would have been easier, like, when I came than to be here for this long. This is the third year now. What I am now, I am completely different. If I met a Congolese who just came today, we don't think the same . . . my heart is completely different to someone who just came.*

For others, the essential questions of where they would go and whom they would live with when they had no remaining family members were central to their anxieties about being returned. Sherriff from Liberia also had worries about how he would be able to access his medication:

*I don't have family there [in Liberia], no dad, no mum, no uncles, no relatives, you know . . . It's gonna be hard for me and I can't . . . maybe I can't get my medication. I have to pay for the prescription and I don't have money, I don't have job. It's gonna be hard for me.*

Several professionals also reflected on the young people's fears about being returned, even when the political situation had settled down. They had made such major adjustments in settling here that the prospect of re-adjusting again to their own countries, but without the support of any family or friends, was just too overwhelming.

A further issue of identity, which was frequently discussed by professionals but not by young people, related to the assumed identities that some young people had taken in order to travel to and enter the UK. Some professionals felt that the stress of maintaining the identity of someone else sometimes caused severe mental health difficulties. They felt that young people might be forced, usually by the agents with whom they had travelled, to pretend they were from a different country or a different cultural group to their own and then felt they could not reveal their true identities once they had arrived. When this happened, they reportedly found it very difficult to settle and adapt to their new environment. While several of the young people we spoke to described entering the UK on false passports, and one temporarily assumed the identity of a much older man, none of them discussed the issue of maintaining a false identity while in the UK.

## Legal and interpreting services

The accounts of dealings with solicitors, reported by asylum-seeking young people, suggest that there is considerable scope to develop better practice in this area. Many talked of solicitors who had failed to deliver applications for further leave to remain on time, had not prepared them for court appearances, failed to make regular contact with them or just provided a very poor and insensitive service.

Once they were able to speak and read English, or once they understood more clearly how the asylum application process worked, a number of young people commented that they were then able to see how poorly their case had been presented to the Home Office by the first solicitor to work with them. The quality of this initial statement made to the Home Office through a solicitor is particularly significant as it becomes the basis of their asylum claim. Yet a number of young people said that the importance of this initial immigration interview was not properly explained to them. Worrying about what they had said on their arrival, and whether or not they had presented information in a way that would help their claim, was a common source of stress among the young people interviewed.

Finding a good solicitor was another worry and in most cases young people had no idea whether the one they were using was any good or not. Social workers might give young people a list of solicitors and help to make the initial contact with them, but their role rarely seemed to extend beyond this. Although legal advice for children and young people seeking asylum is provided by a group of franchised firms selected by the Legal Services Commission on the basis of particular criteria, the experiences recounted by young people in our study suggests significant variation in the quality of service they received; some young people would have liked social workers to provide clearer guidance on accessing and using the services of solicitors.

There were many examples of the problems that inadequate legal support had created for young people seeking asylum. Asif, now aged 15 and from Afghanistan, had appeared in court aged 11 to support an application for indefinite leave to remain in the UK. His solicitor did not turn up and he was left to answer questions completely on his own.

Samuel, from Eritrea, felt that his inability to get early legal advice and support when he arrived at 16 years old had made it far more difficult to make a claim for extending his leave to remain in the UK. Claude talked of his total bemusement when he arrived from Malawi to Heathrow airport during the Christmas holiday, aged 15. For three days he returned each day to the airport where there was no interpreter to help him make his claim for asylum:

> *I didn't get an interpreter. I didn't know what is asylum. And they do present you with papers and you don't know about those kind of things. They ask you to sign and you don't know what those papers mean, which is bad, isn't it?*

Many other young people had faced serious difficulties in identifying a good solicitor and a number had been let down. However, some had better experiences, often at a second or third try. They were able to contrast the more positive experiences of legal support they were receiving from a current lawyer compared with the poor quality service they had previously received. Nasir, aged 18 and from Somalia, commented:

> *The first one [solicitor] was not good really. I would go there and she would say, 'Did I call you?' and when I did have an appointment I would have to wait. So I change solicitor who is really good. He said, 'When you feel anything come and see me.' Really, really, it makes me happy and the other one was making me sad really.*

As well as engaging with solicitors, young people – at least in the early stages of their arrival from Afghanistan – often have to work through interpreters, which exacerbated their worries over what had been said in their initial statement. The quality of interpreters was equally depicted as being very variable. At times they could be supportive of young people, for example, questioning the judgement of social workers who disputed the young person's age, or standing up for them when they first arrived at the airport. However, a number of young people reported very negative experiences of interpreters. They explained how the interpreter was unfriendly or shouted at them, making it very difficult for them to talk about why they had come to seek asylum. Mesaret faced a particularly difficult interaction with an interpreter when she arrived, and believed that the quality of her case for asylum was jeopardised as a result. She explained the problems she had had in presenting her story to a male interpreter from her country:

M: *My case must be strong but I can't explain my situation.*

R: *Why is that?*

M: *My first interpreter was from another community in Ethiopia. I don't like them and I couldn't tell them everything. The interpreter was very poor – he wasn't there to help me, he was there to work. When I signed the papers, the story wasn't right. For example, the name of the political party my family were involved in wasn't translated properly in English. I also felt shy to tell them about the hospital treatment.*

R: *Why did you have hospital treatment?*

M: *I was raped before I came [M began to cry now]. When I first arrived I was very sick. My key worker took me for a check-up and I was told I was pregnant. I had a termination. These things have made me really crazy.*

---

**Implications for policy and practice**

- Young people's immigration status causes extreme anxiety and stress, particularly for those who are in their late teens and nearing the end of their discretionary leave.
- For those young people who have experienced quite severe mental health difficulties, uncertainties surrounding their immigration status are likely to add a further stressful dimension to their situation and may exacerbate their mental health problems.
- The practicalities of where they could return to if deported from the UK were a genuine concern for many young people.
- The quality of the legal support that young people have access to is crucial to ensure that they have a fair chance of being able to remain in the UK. There are currently no clear quality

checks in place to ensure that young people have access to suitably qualified, experienced solicitors who are sensitive to the specific needs of unaccompanied young people seeking asylum.

- The quality of interpreting services that young people have access to is highly variable. Poor interpreting can substantially undermine the strength of a young person's claim to asylum.

# 10 Other sources of support

For young people who arrive unaccompanied to seek asylum in the UK, finding sources of support is likely to be an important factor in promoting their emotional well-being. The young people in the study described a range of such support, drawing both on inner resources such as religious faith, and on external sources such as friends, relatives, community and church groups.

## Religion and faith

Discussions with young people showed that social support was often derived from attending a faith group on a regular basis. It tended to be young women, usually from African countries such as Nigeria, the DRC, Ethiopia and Eritrea, who received the most social support from attending a church, and often a choir and/or youth club that was attached to it. Kiki, a young woman from Eritrea, said that she went to church twice a week, 7–9 pm on Thursdays and 1–5 pm on Sundays, where there was 'lots of singing and Bible stories'. Remi from Nigeria attended church on Wednesdays and Sundays and also choir practice on Saturdays. The church and associated activities served to keep these young people busy and provided them with social support.

Young men, however, did not tend to have the same involvement as young women. Claude, for example, commented:

*I just go to church and hear mass – after that I go home. I don't socialise there, I just go and come home.*

The young people – men and women – who were practising Muslims derived much emotional support and hope from their faith but did not, on the whole, receive the same level of social support from the mosque as the young female Christians did from their churches. Ibrahim, for example, when he was asked if he received support from the mosque, replied:

*No, it is not like the church. It is not like your Father and you talk –
we just go there and pray; we don't need to talk to them. We just finish
and go. I don't know other people at the mosque.*

While faith groups, especially Christian ones, provided a source of social
support for many young people, the importance of the spiritual side of
religion was emphasised by many. Some young people spoke about
'God's will', 'God's wish' and resorting to a 'greater being' when talking
about their lives, a belief that clearly gave them hope for the future. Kiki,
for example, took several pictures of the Bible, when invited by the
researcher to take photos of things that were important to her, and said
that she spent an hour every day reading it. Aliya from Somalia took a
picture of the Koran and said that she spent time memorising the chapters,
which 'helps me'. Like others, she found comfort in her religion:

*It is comfort . . . it makes me feel that we are just here temporary . . .
we are going to die. It's sad sometimes but when you see the Koran you
see that it is true – in the end we are going to go back . . . I don't feel
sad because I feel we are going to die one day and leave behind all
these troubles and all this pain.*

Claude went on to describe how, despite all the loss and grief he had
experienced, it was his faith in God that helped him cope:

*I trust my belief in God in everything which I do. When you believe,
you don't really feel lonely. I feel like when I go to church I listen to
music, some prayer, I just feel like me. I forget everything. It's my
counselling, isn't it?*

## Friends

Perhaps not surprisingly, the vast majority of the young people we spoke
to cited friends as their closest source of support. Most of the professionals we interviewed also felt that young people, in the main, saw
friends as crucial to their well-being. Eritrean and Ethiopian girls
described particularly close friendships with other Eritreans and
Ethiopians, often cooking and eating together and sometimes attending

church together. Similarly, Chinese young women described having close networks of friends and were frequently described by professionals as being very supportive of one another.

However, one of the most common themes from our discussions was the need for young people to maintain a sense of privacy, and in many cases secrecy, in their relationships with friends. As Hellen explained:

*If I am sad, I can talk to friends about normal things. There are some things I don't talk about – private things.*

And, as Thierry, aged 16 and from Burundi, said about his friends:

*They know enough, they know what I allow them to know.*

Many spoke about their need to keep their asylum-seeking status a secret from friends, which had obvious implications for having close and trusting friendships. As Maryam explained:

*It's strange because I feel they [university people] are my closest friends, but then they're not because they don't know about me. It's good to be able to be who you are without hiding bits and pieces of your life.*

Maryam felt that this need for secrecy resulted in her avoiding social situations, as she did not want to lie to people:

*I don't always feel like making conversations with people. I don't want to lie to them but if they ask me something, I prefer not to make conversations because I'd rather not lie. So it's kind of hard to socialise sometimes. You'd rather not say anything than lie. I spend a lot of time alone.*

Patrick, aged 15 and from the DRC, explained how he felt the need to present himself as two different people, in different ways for different audiences:

*You don't really get to explain your friends that you are an asylum seeker – unless they are. But if they are not asylum seekers also then you just come up with a story that you are living with your aunty or something . . . There's a lot of pretence about what's really going on.*

William, also from the DRC, similarly explained that he could not tell his friends he was an asylum seeker; instead, because he speaks French, he tells them that he is from France.

Some young people described how their friendships had been disrupted, in many cases removing their main source of support. This was either because they had been dispersed to another city in Britain, as was the case with Daisy from China, or because they had had to move to another area in London, for example, after leaving foster care, which meant that their friends now lived a long distance away. This was particularly an issue for Miguel from Angola, who had to travel across London on a regular basis to meet up with his friends. The cost of travel and the time involved, when many were in college and/or had young children, made travelling to see friends in another area very difficult for a number of young people.

Friends could not always be relied on for support and some young men in particular described feeling let down at times by friends, who were not there when they needed them or whom they felt only got in touch when they wanted a favour.

## Relatives

A number of the young people who participated in the study, most commonly boys and young men from Afghanistan, had some contact with relatives in the UK. This contact – often with uncles and older siblings – was an important contributing factor to the young person's overall sense of well-being. Through these blood relations, they were able to maintain links and memories with their home country, culture and language, and were sometimes able to hear news from family left behind.

Yasir, an 18 year-old from Afghanistan, had started living with one of his two uncles, both of whom were resident in Britain when his foster placement had broken down. He felt that if he needed emotional support, he would be able to talk to one of them. Miguel, aged 18 and from Angola, had two sisters in the UK and lived with one of them after leaving foster care. He identified his sisters as his main source of emotional support. Thirteen-year-old Zalmai from Afghanistan went to stay with his uncle on alternate weekends. He told us how his uncle took him to Afghan restaurants, spoke Pashtu with him and accompanied him to the mosque. Through his uncle, he occasionally received news from Afghanistan:

*My uncle is in touch [with Afghanistan]. We see things on the news and worry so it is a relief when he gives me news of them.*

Those young people who did not have any contact with relatives either in the UK or from their country of origin were more likely to describe feelings of isolation and loneliness.

## Community groups

A small number of young people in the study spoke about the contribution that community groups had made to their lives, some in a positive way and others in a more negative sense. Nanu from Eritrea explained how she had gone to the Ethiopian community for advice and support and through them was put in contact with the Connexions service. She was happy with the intervention of the community group, especially as she felt she had not received the advice and support she needed about accessing education and childcare support from social services.

However, other young people were more critical of community groups, who, in their view, mirrored the divisions of the country from which they had fled and so were not interested in helping them. Although Ibrahim, for example, lived in an area heavily populated by other Pakistani people, he felt that they were not helpful to him because of his asylum-seeking status:

*No, they are not helping, they are not interested . . . they are British born, they are different thinking. I am not happy with them.*

Similarly, Simeon was very critical of the Somali community groups he had been in touch with. He said that he did not feel related to them and that he was not supported because of his asylum-seeking status. Instead of being helped and respected, he said, he 'felt like an outcast'. One personal adviser we spoke to echoed this view, giving an example of a Somali young man who did not want to get involved with Somali community groups in the UK. When asked why, he said that he left Somalia to get away from the factions among groups, and that he was being presented with some of the same problems here as those he had left behind.

One young woman, Chrisna from the DRC, felt that she did not want contact with the Congolese community attached to her church in case she heard 'bad news' about her family from them. She said that she preferred to see people from different backgrounds so that she could avoid the possibility of finding out the 'truth' which she felt that she was not presently strong enough to cope with.

---

### Implications for policy and practice

- Many young people derive support from their friendship groups. Placement changes experienced by young people risk isolating them from important supportive networks and this needs to be taken into account when decisions are made about where asylum-seeking children and young people should live.

- Professionals need to exercise caution about automatically linking children and young people with community organisations. While some such groups are clearly supportive, others may be less so, and it is important not to make assumptions about the usefulness and suitability of such organisations for all young people.

- Religion and faith were important for the majority of young people participating in the research, but the extent to which they wanted to engage in church and faith communities varied enormously. Many young men, for example, described their faith as something quite private which they wished to practise on their own.

- Ensuring that young people are able to link up with family relatives wherever possible is very important, since they may be a major source of emotional and cultural support.

---

- All young people seeking asylum who have been separated from family members should be given information about the International Red Cross tracing service which may be able to assist them in re-establishing contact with their families.

# 11 Resilience and the ways in which young people cope and adapt

In this chapter, we discuss the range of ways in which children and young people described coping and adapting to life in the UK in the face of a range of anxieties and other emotional difficulties. Many described times in which they coped well, and times when everything became too much for them and they required additional support. Health, social care and other professionals made the same observation. Despite numerous difficulties and enormous adversity, however, many young people had managed to achieve a great deal since arriving in the UK and it is important that their strengths and resilience are also acknowledged.

## Adapting to life in the UK

Despite the difficulties that young people described with respect to their arrival in the UK and their legal status, many spoke to us about their joy and relief at being in Britain (see also Hopkins and Hill, 2006). Young people used words like 'feeling safe' and 'secure' and having 'freedom' in this country. Some, like Azyeb, aged 18 and from Eritrea, expressed gratitude to the British government for the support they had received:

> *Thank you to this country, thank you to this government – they did everything for me. I hope one day I will be able to work for it and pay tax for this country ... I think it is a really, really, really good country – I don't think that anywhere can compare with this country, I believe.*

Nasir, aged 18 and from Somalia, spoke about how 'wonderful' it was that he did not hear gun shots in Britain and how 'strange' it was to not see people carrying a gun. William from the DRC commented that despite everything he had been through, he felt able to laugh here:

*In this country people are good, they are nice, they make me laugh. I can have fun, I can laugh. That has changed my life a lot . . . it changed my life a lot.*

Similarly, Chrisna said she loved the UK because of all the people from different nationalities she had met and the opportunity she now had to learn about different cultures. She commented:

*I like a lot of things about the UK. I feel more secure here. It's like my home here. I like being here.*

Several young people said how they especially enjoyed the company of older people in this country and that they had learned a lot from them. One youth worker also described how one of the young men he worked with would always get off his bus a stop early so that he could accompany an elderly person to their flat since he enjoyed their company a great deal.

Young people made references to how different their lives were here in the UK compared to where they had come from. Simeon from Somalia loved to travel around London on buses and the tube, just observing life. He said:

*As a child I was ill and my dad had to carry me. We couldn't afford transport so it was a very, very long journey. I have images in my head about it. I was seven and there was no service road. Ambulances were only for the rich in Somalia. It's easy to get around here, to visit each other. I realise I won't have to put my children through that.*

Kenneh from Liberia talked of how he missed the food from his home and how he disliked English food. He particularly missed the staple food in Liberia called *manoc* (casava) and described in detail how you have to let it grow and then let the sun ripen it properly for two more weeks before cooking and eating it. Joy, from Nigeria, said that she missed 'fresh food all the time, not chemical food – I am exhausted with that'. Ajani from Afghanistan also described how, although they never had much to eat in his village, all the food that he ate was always fresh, picked straight from the trees or dug from the soil. This was something that he really missed.

Some young people indicated that the values and norms that they had arrived with, and their expectations of how their lives would develop, had begun to change. Thierry's views about marriage are indicative of this:

*I used to think that I'd get married when I was 16 'cos my dad got married at 17. So I grew up thinking that I would get a wife at 16 or 17. Now I've seen that there's more to life than getting married when you're young.*

Several young people either commented on notions of childhood here in the UK or contrasted their own childhoods to ones they observed here. Sherriff from Liberia described how, from a young age, he had to wake up at 5am every day to help his father farm their land. Similarly, Amir from Iran had herded sheep since he was a small boy. Thierry commented on how young people from his own country, Burundi, were more mature than young people he met here:

*[Here] people have different minds too, minds are more grown up in my country. Here their minds are still on their PS2 Play Station. People say to me 'you are different', even girls I go out with. They say I'm not usual, the way I treat them. My friends try and cheat girls but I treat girls with respect.*

Joy from Nigeria also commented on childhood and youth here and how it was very different to back home. She reflected:

*'Cos that's why people here find me really difficult sometimes. They say, 'I don't think Joy is 13, she behave really mature you know – no 13-year-old behave like that.' How they gonna behave like that when you feed them here every minute just like they do a newborn baby? How are they going to learn . . . they don't even know how to wash their clothes or cook rice . . . as I can cook for a party, for a hundred people . . . but these people find me so difficult . . .*

Malashu gave a very specific example of how cultural differences affected the way she had responded to social workers:

*Sometimes . . . in my culture, if you go to someone's house, they offer you food to eat, it's respectful to say 'no' at first and then they say it again and you say 'yes'. Here, some social workers, if you say some-thing like 'no', they just take it as a 'no' and they don't really know the culture. Sometimes it'd be nice if they knew the culture.*

Asif, who had arrived aged 10 from Afghanistan and was now 15, tried to capture how different life was here in the UK to back home, as well as the complexities of his feelings about being here:

*The lifestyle here compared to over there is much different . . . you can't get all the stuff you need there and over here, thank God, I have everything I need. Well, obviously it's better living with your own family and you feel better because you can say whatever, you can do whatever, but living over there is your homeland, and you don't feel like you are far from anyone. You've got everyone with you, but over here you do think that you are far away from your family and you haven't seen them for five years. And yeah . . . it's easy to live here, but it's also difficult.*

Although some young people found themselves better off and with far greater access to resources than they had been used to before coming to the UK, there were others from wealthy families who had had to adapt on many levels. These young people sometimes commented on the poor quality of their housing and accommodation, and the fact that they had to learn to do many tasks that they would never normally have done for themselves, such as cooking, cleaning and washing.

Despite often feeling safer in the UK, many young people also spoke of the difficulties they had faced making relationships with British people. Many found the British reserve a culture shock and had been surprised that they could not get close to British people and were rarely invited to their homes. As Mahamat from Chad explained:

*You can't get a social life in this country, you don't have a connection with anybody, you feel lonely and this is really hard. How can you make friends in this country? . . . Even your neighbours never say 'hi'.*

Zemar, aged 20 from Afghanistan, echoed this observation when he described British society as lacking 'interaction' and being 'a really individualistic society'. He went on to explain that he thought there was a 'culture of indifference to other human beings in this society and it's very disastrous'.

Kenneh, aged 17 and from Liberia, had also found it difficult to make friends with 'English' people because of cultural differences. He said that he never sees children and young people playing outside nor do any boys ask him to their house, with the result that 'I have never been to someone's home'.

Joy, now 17 but who has lived in the UK since she was 13, focused on the difference in people's willingness to be sociable compared to Nigeria, her home country:

> *This country teaches you how to stay on your own because even your neighbours, they don't really talk to you. But in Nigeria, we communicate – we really do communicate. You know you can just walk into anybody's home and just ask for food . . . Here you can't do that. And I do kinda miss that kind of life, 'cos it's really free.*

She went on to talk about how being with people was also very different. In Nigeria, people were more tactile with each other, friends put arms around each other. Here, on the other hand, she said she had been labelled a "lesbian" when she had openly demonstrated affection for other women.

Mahlet talked about how one of the hardest things she found was the unpleasant way in which people related to each other here, whereas people in her own country, in her opinion, did not treat each other in this way – shouting at each other, hurling abuse. Ajani from Afghanistan could not understand why people were always rushing everywhere. He also felt that younger people lacked respect for their elders and had too much freedom. Other young people commented on the over-emphasis on money and possessions and thought that people did not care enough or find enough time for each other.

The ability to speak English was clearly a factor in helping young people seeking asylum to adapt to their new situation. As mentioned earlier, most were able to communicate quite fluently in English within a relatively short time of arriving here. However, language acquisition did vary according to their age and their placement. Younger children placed with English-speaking families generally developed a fluency in English quickly. Namir, aged 11 at the time of the research, had come from Afghanistan at nine and explained how he felt 'sad' when he arrived because he could not speak English. He learned it from another boy placed with the same foster carer and from the TV. Houmam, aged 16, had arrived from Syria just six months before he took part in the research. He described difficulties that he was still having in terms of expressing himself, and said that although he had some friends:

*I don't want to talk to them because of my English. I can't tell them what I want to tell them so I don't talk much.*

Older young people seeking asylum were usually placed in semi-independent or independent accommodation, sometimes with others speaking their mother tongue. However, access to language learning (ESOL) classes was described very positively by young people, as was the additional language support that they received in schools and colleges.

Chinese young people – in our study they were all female – seemed to have had the greatest difficulty in terms of language acquisition, and this consequently limited their access to wider curricula. Whereas young people from other countries usually spent the first year concentrating on ESOL (sometimes combined with other studies) and then moved on to other courses in subjects that interested them, the Chinese young women we spoke to, and others that we were told about, tended to remain in ESOL classes for much longer. The linguistic leap from Mandarin or Cantonese to English is undoubtedly greater than for speakers of some other languages. Another factor, however, was that the Chinese were very commonly placed together in shared houses where they would speak Mandarin or Chinese, share similar food and keep to themselves. Some professionals commented on how the young Chinese people in particular had developed a very close-knit and supportive network to which they readily welcomed newcomers. It appeared likely that this might partly have stemmed from a sense of isolation and difficulty in integrating as a result of the language barrier.

Many of the young people who participated in the study revealed stories of stigma and discrimination as a result of their asylum-seeking status. Commonly used words to describe how they felt in the UK as asylum-seeking young people included 'outsiders' and 'outcasts'. Some described negative reactions from members of the public, influenced by media portrayals of asylum seekers, and it was common for young people to feel the need to keep their asylum-seeking status secret from friends and acquaintances. Many of the professionals we spoke to identified the stigma facing asylum-seeking young people as a huge issue in their welfare. One social worker we interviewed said she wanted to have the opportunity to say how proud she and other colleagues were of the unaccompanied young people she worked with, and how they needed to be given a chance:

> *The roughly general opinion about asylum seekers in this country needs to change if we really want to help them – we have to give them the chance, to know the capability of the young person. They will be so useful to society if we give them the chance.*

## Ways of coping

The need to keep busy, distracting themselves from thinking about sad things, came up again and again in our discussions with young people. As Remi explained, when she was asked how she copes with difficult things:

> *I just forget about it. I just stop thinking about it. If I keep thinking about it, it will stay there and I wouldn't be able to do whatever. So life goes on, I just get on with my life. I just take my mind off it.*

Similarly, Zalmai, from Afghanistan, explained how he copes when he is sad:

> *I try and forget – I do something else to be busy.*

Many young people cited taking part in sport as a means of helping them cope with sad memories and anxieties. This was one way of escaping, of helping them not to think about their past lives and difficulties. As Houmam, from Syria, commented:

*I love to play football. When I play football, I forget everything.*

Similarly, Thierry from Burundi explained how playing basketball made him feel so much better and prevented him from 'thinking too much'.

For some, like Peter from Uganda, playing sport was a way of "connecting" to other people. He felt that even if people were negative towards him because of his asylum-seeking status, then being good at sport was a way of compensating and showing that he deserved to be treated better.

Sporting activities pursued by young people included both team sports such as football, basketball and cricket, which were more likely to be cited by young men, and more solitary activities such as running, swimming and going to the gym, which were more often mentioned by young women. Young people took part in sports at a variety of venues, such as school, college, local leisure centres and in local parks and streets.

Enjoyment of sport was more likely to be cited by young people in foster care placements. Many young people living in independent housing placements, with access to just £45 or so per week, spoke about their frustration at not being able to participate in sport because of the costs involved. Sheriff, from Liberia, explained how he wanted to do swimming or weight training in his free time but that it was too expensive for him to do so. Houmam expressed frustration at not being able to do much during the long school holidays:

*I'd like to go to the gym but it's closed. It's summer and I have nothing to do. The foster family are going on holiday but I can't go with them as I haven't got a passport. I would like to go to a football club in summer but I don't know where. They say they are all closed all summer.*

Chrisna explained how even going for a swim cost her £7 each time so she could rarely afford it. Membership of her local gym would cost £30 a month, which she definitely could not afford. Mesaret likewise said that going to the gym or swimming would really help her emotionally, but that the cost was too prohibitive.

A number of young men talked of how they had done really well at football and had been scouted to play in the junior teams of national league teams. However, in each case, they were unable to continue with the coaching because of their immigration status and the fact that they did not have indefinite leave to remain in the UK.

Several of the professionals interviewed felt that access to leisure and youth activities for young people seeking asylum was too limited, or was restricted to specialist services targeted at them rather than integrated activities where young people could socialise with others from different backgrounds.

The need to be outside, walking in the park or in the snow, was identified by a number of young people as contributing to their emotional well-being. As Aliya explained:

> *I like long boats on the river. I like the green sites, the flowers that grow there. When I am sad, I picture myself sitting in a chair near the park . . . and you know, I discovered that if you got a plant and you water, you feel good when it grows.*

Mesaret from Ethiopia had just moved to a new placement when we spoke to her for the study. Her room in the shared house was very small and the house was situated on a very busy, noisy, main road. When asked about things that helped her to cope, she replied:

> *I liked the views in my last place. I like the trees and the forest. I felt like it was my home. When the children played outside, I felt like I'm back at home.*

Simeon, aged 20 and from Somalia, also identified nature as promoting his emotional well-being:

> *When I feel depressed, I walk in the park. When I feel trapped, I go and take a deep breath. It makes me feel good – the lake, the nature. It is where I chill out. When I have memories . . . I can feel trapped, I need to get out. It makes me calm down.*

Undertaking voluntary work and helping others was another coping strategy that some young people adopted. Zemar, aged 20, described a project he was working on with another Afghan student to raise money to send back to Afghanistan to build libraries for girls. Peter from Uganda was also involved in "charity work" such as working with older people. This voluntary work, he said, had helped him 'find other solutions', 'open up his eyes to British culture' and had given him greater confidence. Saba, a 14-year-girl from Eritrea, spoke about how she and other young people at school were making cakes and selling them for charity. She explained that she wanted 'to build a better world' and do 'something better'.

## Personal strength and resilience

Despite experiencing severe trauma and displacement, many of the young people involved in our study appeared to be coping well emotionally and had not, so far, succumbed to mental health problems requiring medical intervention. This finding is in keeping with earlier work with refugee and asylum-seeking young people (e.g. Kline and Mone, 2003; Kohli and Mather, 2003; Wallin and Ahlstrom, 2005). The study participants who, overall, appeared to be coping shared an approach to their life that included a positive outlook, optimism, hope and the belief that things would turn out better for them in the end. Mahamat from Chad described his outlook in the following way, attributing his strength to his patience:

> *I am a strong person, I have a strong mind . . . I am not easy to get lost at all. When I do things, I always think, I always ask – every time there is always a solution – it might take a long time but there is always a solution. Sometimes people think they have a problem and their life is finished, but life is never finished. It depends on the people and how patient they are. I am always patient.*

Zemar explained that his strategy for coping included thinking of a person 'who is worse off than you' and for being 'grateful' for what he had. Others felt that having high ambitions, aspirations and dreams gave them hope for the future and helped them to cope. As Amir, an 18-year-old from Iran, commented:

> *I think to myself I never lose the future, I tell myself you can't lose the future . . . so I will get a nice everything.*

And Yemi from Nigeria explained her coping strategy in the following way:

*My dreams . . . I want to be this, I want to be that . . . that keeps me going.*

Some young people shared their belief that "anything is possible" and others spoke about their wish to change the world, an aspiration which clearly helped them to cope with adversity. As 17-year-old Malashu from Eritrea said:

*I want to change the world. I would hope to work for the UN and help make the world a better place . . . to get rid of all dictators.*

Patrick from the DRC also felt that the key to coping was to be accepting of what is happening and to learn to see the positive side to any event:

*When you just make negative things positive, what you do is you don't worry any more . . . What you do is just think. I think about things . . . what decision I should take, what risks I should take.*

Although young people under 18 who seek asylum alone in the UK are regarded as looked after children, several professionals highlighted the fact that those seeking asylum differ in many ways from other young people in care. One LAC nurse, for example, commented:

*When I compare them to local looked after children, they seem to be so much more determined . . . able . . . they just seem to want to make something of themselves; they are very very able. It's like looking at two completely different sets of young people. Local kids just feel like they are battered, have been through the system, but unaccompanied children and young people just keep fighting on, working hard.*

In fact, there are both similarities and differences in the situations of young people seeking asylum and others within the care system. We return in the concluding chapter to the similarities that give wider relevance to many of the findings of this study. However, one difference that is particularly relevant to discussions of mental health and emotional well-being is that, although both groups appear to have much higher levels of mental health difficulties than do young people in the general population, the types of difficulties they experience may differ. A national survey of the mental health of young people looked after by local authorities in England (Melzer *et al*, 2003) reported a high level of mental health disorders (49% among 11–15-year-olds, compared to 11% among this age group in the general population). The most common category among looked after children was "conduct disorders" (40% of looked after 11–15-year-olds), with far fewer (12%) recorded as having an "emotional disorder" such as anxiety or depression. Although we did not attempt in our study to make such clinical diagnoses, it would seem that mental health difficulties among children and young people seeking asylum, contrary to the findings from the national survey of looked after children and young people in general, are more likely to manifest as emotional rather than conduct problems.

## Pregnancy and parenthood

The final issue which we consider in relation to young people's adaptation to life in the UK is that of pregnancy and parenthood. Many professionals whom we spoke to highlighted the frequency of pregnancy among young women seeking asylum on their own. Although there were some instances when young women arrived pregnant (usually as a result of rape), many of the young women reportedly became pregnant soon after arriving.

The reasons given for this varied. Some professionals associated pregnancy with a lack of knowledge among young asylum seekers about sexual health and how their bodies work. Others felt that becoming pregnant was a way of forming new attachments, providing them with status and a focus in life. While many young women faced with a pregnancy went on to have their babies, some requested repeated terminations despite being advised about contraceptive services. One or two professionals felt that young people were under the misconception that having a baby would somehow benefit their claim for asylum. Most professionals, however, did not share this view.

There were important cultural factors that appeared to come into play with respect to pregnancy and parenthood among this group of young people which are, as yet, not well understood. For example, while many of the young women were considered to be "single", one GP pointed out that in their own eyes they are "married" since they have had a child with someone. This was particularly thought to be the case for young women coming from the Horn of Africa.

Another nurse practitioner working in general practice was certain that the pregnancies were intentional rather than "accidents". She felt the main reason was because having a baby offered young women 'status, stability, something to love and giving them a focus'. She also commented that while other young mothers from the UK she had come across struggled to bring up their children, in her experience, this was not the case with unaccompanied young women. Not only that, they also frequently remained in education and had high aspirations for themselves and their children. She could see many positive benefits to parenthood for young women who had experienced being wrenched from all family and social ties.

One of the unexpected findings of this study was the number of asylum-seeking young people who were either pregnant, had had a child or had fathered a child. Nine of the 54 participants, including two young men, already had a child or were about to have one. Another young woman reported that she had been pregnant but had terminated the pregnancy.

Having a baby had different associations for the young people to whom we spoke. Mireille from Cameroon talked of how her baby helped her cope with her past experiences and the problems that she was now facing:

> Before, I didn't have anything. I used to live just like that, without knowing what was going to happen. I don't know what's happened to my dad, mum. I don't know where they are, but I have my baby now. Now I feel I have something to do, I am important to someone. I have to feed him and take him to the park. Before I used to live like that, I would eat because I had to.

Twenty-one-year-old Rakeb, who is Eritrean and arrived from Ethiopia when she was 15, referred to her child as the 'only happiness I have . . .

he is my family now'. Joy had become pregnant at the age of 14, less than a year after arriving in the UK. She had decided to terminate the pregnancy, but later on had doubts about whether or not she had done the right thing.

Nanu, now aged 20, arrived from Eritrea at the age of 16. She was six months pregnant as a result of being raped in Eritrea. Despite being advised by her social worker to terminate the pregnancy or give up the baby for adoption, she decided to have the baby and, at the time of the interview, he was four years old.

Nancy, aged 19 and from China, had become pregnant after arriving in the UK. She said that it had not been planned but that she had stayed together with her boyfriend, although neither of them knew whether or not they could remain in the UK. She commented that it would be very difficult for her to return to China as an unmarried mother. The baby would have no status and would not be able to study or go to school.

William from the DRC had a daughter who was three months old at the time of the research. Although he also claimed that the pregnancy was not planned, he felt very positive about being a father:

*It's a good thing anyway because I am alone, I always feel lonely and when I see my daughter, it is a big thing for me. I know I am too young for it but it helps me to not have all them stresses about my family or all them things . . . That's just life.*

Innocent from Nigeria, who had experienced very severe mental health difficulties, described how the fact that his partner would be having a baby soon had been a positive boost to his mental health:

*Although I still have lots of worries, it's like, oh, the baby's coming so I have to pull myself together . . . That's really helping me . . . it helps me a lot.*

There are clearly many issues relating to pregnancy and parenthood among asylum-seeking young people that would benefit from further exploration and analysis in future research.

## Implications for policy and practice

- Asylum-seeking young people, given the right support, are able to achieve a great deal once they arrive in the UK.
- Opportunities for sport, leisure and social activities are very beneficial for the emotional well-being of these young people. There is a need for more, and more affordable, leisure opportunities, particularly for young people in independent and semi-independent accommodation who have the least access to these services since they cannot afford to access them.
- Many young people face elements of racism and stigma from the general public as a result of their asylum status in the UK.
- Some young people find it more difficult than others to adapt culturally, and find life in the UK very different to that in their own countries. Opportunities to integrate young people into community services and events, rather than generating activities solely for asylum-seeking young people, are likely to facilitate this cultural transition.
- Pregnancy and parenthood appear to be widespread among some groups of young asylum seekers. This is an area of work which requires further research to find out more about the motivations and reasons for early pregnancy and the types of implications for appropriate preventive and support services.

# 12 Conclusions

This exploratory study has considered a wide range of factors that either promote or negatively impact on the emotional well-being of unaccompanied young people seeking asylum in the UK. The use of an open-ended and qualitative methodology allowed a number of key themes to emerge from the data.

As outlined at the end of each chapter, the findings from this work have important implications for the range of services that unaccompanied young people seeking asylum are likely to come into contact with. These include primary, secondary and tertiary care services, social care services, education, immigration and legal services, benefits agencies – including income support and housing – and informal and community networks and services. The research elicited clear indications of where policy and practice governing all these areas of support could function more effectively to promote the well-being of unaccompanied young people seeking asylum, minimise the impact of the more negative experiences they have endured and harness the enormous personal resources and resilience of many remarkable young people.

**While some of the findings are specific to young people seeking asylum, there are a number of similarities between the situations of such young people and looked after children more generally, which suggest that the findings may have wider relevance.** For example, young people coming into the local authority care system will also have experienced trauma and difficulties, may have little contact with their family of origin, and may find it hard to trust the professionals around them or to ask for help (Mental Health Foundation, 2002). Frequent changes of placement and poor inter-agency communication have been shown to create difficulties in gaining access to adequate health care, and despite the high level of need, there are often long waiting lists for services such as CAMHS (Ward *et al*, 2002). As with young people seeking asylum, young people leaving care often face significant practical and social problems and may be unable to afford leisure and recreational facilities. Limited housing options often mean that care leavers are placed in bed and breakfast accommodation, with little support or preparation for independent living. It has been noted by one psychiatrist experienced in working with such groups that 'the impact [of these practical and social problems] on their mental health cannot be stressed enough' (Vostanis, 2005, p 112). Young people who have not been in care but have experienced disrupted and difficult lives may fare even worse than those who have been looked after, since they also have a high level of mental health difficulties but no entitlement to "leaving care" services (Cameron *et al*, 2007).

## The significance of age, gender, ethnicity and country of origin

One of the original aims of our analysis was to elicit the significance of age, gender, ethnicity and country of origin in relation to the factors promoting or negatively impacting on the emotional well-being of children and young people seeking asylum. A central theme emerging from the analysis, however, was the uniqueness of the lives, experiences, circumstances and personal characteristics of each of the young people in the study. Many professionals also stressed the importance of working with each young person as an individual, and this study clearly reiterates the need for this approach. This said, the study did elicit some important broad findings concerning how age, gender and country of origin appear to affect how young people seeking asylum coped with life in the UK. These can be summarised as follows:

- **Younger participants were less likely to display emotional distress than older young people**. This may have been due to a combination of factors, such as being exposed to fewer traumatic events prior to their departure or being better protected from traumatic events, living in supportive foster care arrangements and having more time to settle and adapt without having the additional stress or uncertainty about their future status in the UK.

- **The majority of young people who took part in this study arrived at the age of 15 (20%) or 16 (30%) years old**. This broadly fits the national pattern of unaccompanied young people arriving in the UK.

Not all young people were given discretionary leave to remain up until the age of 18 years, with a number only being granted one year's leave initially and then having to re-apply to the Home Office for further leave to remain. As a result, at the time of interview, the majority of young people were in the process of either making an application to remain in the UK or waiting for the outcome of their application. This was at a time when young people were being told that they may wait up to five years for a decision to be made on their asylum/ leave to remain applications. The most immediate concern and cause for anxiety for the older young people we spoke to, therefore, was about their immigration status.

- **At the time of their participation in the study, the majority of young people (60%) were aged 18 years and over, similar to the age profile of all young people seeking asylum in the local authority hosting the research.** Those aged 18 years and over commonly expressed high levels of anxiety about what would happen in their future. This caused uncertainties regarding not only their immigration status but also in relation to education, housing and employment. These young people described difficulties in opening a bank account, getting a financial loan, getting a driving licence or securing part-time employment. Some young people were 21 years old and still uncertain about their future in the UK.

- **Young women seemed far more likely to express their emotional feelings and support needs to social care and other professionals than did young men.** It appears likely that most young men have been socialised at a young age to appear to cope, be responsible and to not show their feelings openly.

- **From the study sample, young women were far more likely than young men to report having been subjected to sexual violence** either prior to leaving their countries of origin or during their journeys.

- **With regard to ethnicity and country of origin, some groups – in particular Chinese, Eritrean and Ethiopian young women – appear to develop strong and supportive networks.** Young people from these countries newly arriving in the UK were reportedly welcomed into these groups and offered support. The availability of this support network may be partly as a result of the large numbers of young people arriving from these countries within the authority participating in the research.

## Impact of placement factors

Another key focus of the study was to try and explore how far placement factors affected the emotional well-being and mental health of unaccompanied young people seeking asylum. The main findings in relation to this question are as follows:

- **Foster placements, when they work well, can provide important all-round support for young people seeking asylum alone.** Several older young people described still having very close relationships with former foster carers, whom they identified as continuing sources of support with many aspects of their lives, even though they no longer lived with them.

- **When foster placements broke down, this was often related to the expectations that the carers had of young people or that young people had of foster carers.** Young people in their older teens may have had to grow up far more quickly than their non-asylum-seeking peers and as such may present themselves differently to other young people. This could create friction and difficulties within foster placements.

- **Young people in semi-supported accommodation reported valuing the additional assistance they received either from an allocated social worker or key worker.** Most young people who did have access to a key worker were limited to four hours support each week.

- **Young women participating in the study who had children valued the support that they received in mother and baby units**, both from social workers and from the other young women with whom they were placed.

- **Young people in independent accommodation were, unsurprisingly, more likely to describe times when they felt isolated or**

**lacked the support they needed**. This was particularly the case when, on reaching 18 years, they had been moved to different accommodation which was often away from friends with whom they might have been living for a number of years.

- **Some accommodation appeared to be inappropriate for young people's needs** and several young people reported not feeling "safe" in the place where they were living.

- **The quality of the independent accommodation that was observed by researchers varied enormously**. In some cases, young people had access to shared spaces in the house where they could eat as well as cook together and a separate living space for relaxation and communal living. In other cases, young people had very basic shared cooking amenities and described having to eat alone in their bedrooms since there was no shared communal space to eat.

## Impact of other factors

The third focus of the research analysis was in relation to wider factors that promoted or negatively impacted on the emotional well-being of unaccompanied young people. Over and above those factors discussed above in relation to placement, age and immigration status, these can be summarised as follows:

- **Unaccompanied young people seeking asylum, particularly those aged 15 years and over, frequently reported a wide range of emotional well-being and mental health needs**. These ranged from day-to-day anxieties and worries through to acute depression and at times severe mental illness. Conduct disorders, the most common mental health issue among looked after children, appeared, at least in our study sample, to be far less common.

- **Some young people clearly coped better than others**. Having distractions such as sporting and leisure facilities, spending time in the library or studying, attending a church, mosque or temple and other related activities, and spending time with friends all appeared to promote a sense of well-being and attachment for young people.

- **Despite the fact that many young people described quite serious levels of anxiety, difficulties in accessing support through primary care services were frequent**. Several young people described concerns about what they considered to be the inappropriate use of medication for symptoms which they felt could not be "cured". Similarly, not being listened to, or not knowing how to access primary care services to express their needs were also described as creating problems.

- **Although counselling services were often offered to young people when they arrived in the UK, this form of help was not well understood by them and often had deeply stigmatising associations**. This prevented some of the young people in the study from accessing counselling or similar therapies from which they might have benefited. Conversely, some young people who had become emotionally very unwell and had been provided with counselling services, did appear to have benefited from these. Finding ways to present young people with more culturally appropriate ways of accessing therapeutic support should clearly be a high priority.

- **Accessing and staying in education was extremely important to the emotional well-being of the majority of the young people we spoke to**. This provided them with a focus both for the present and for the future. Making sure that they are able to make the best use of educational opportunities while they are in the UK requires careful assessment, appropriate placements and equitable access to opportunities for further education through support mechanisms such as student loans.

- **Given the central importance of their immigration status, young people require access to accessible and good quality legal support services**. They often described having received poor quality legal advice from solicitors and from interpreters engaged in asylum claims procedures. Young people reported needing more support and guidance in identifying good solicitors and in accessing legal services.

While some of the issues reported on have been addressed elsewhere in previous studies of unaccompanied asylum-seeking young people (e.g.

Fazel and Stein, 2003; Kohli and Mather, 2003; Kohli, 2005; Wade *et al*, 2005), the present research offers a variety of new insights into specific needs in relation to their emotional well-being and mental health.

Firstly, by giving primacy to the views and opinions of young people themselves, we have highlighted some important areas for future policy and practice across a number of disciplines. Secondly, unlike some earlier studies, this research has had a strong focus on the specific issues faced by young people during the transition to adulthood and the implications that this has for their future. These are essentially young people who have spent a number of their formative years in the UK and who face the prospect of returning to countries of origin which in many cases have become alien to them. It would be helpful if professionals were clearer about their roles during this transition, since currently many young people describe not being given the support they require at this stage. Thirdly, we have been able to provide some distinctive insights into some of the understandings that young people from different cultures have in relation to areas of health termed "emotional well-being" or "mental health". These understandings have implications for care and support across the spectrum of health services, from primary care through to Tier-3 and Tier-4 mental health services.

There is an ever-shifting policy landscape in relation to all refugee and asylum seekers in the UK, and more specifically for unaccompanied children and young people seeking asylum. The New Asylum Model, described in the introduction to this book, and suggested measures to reconfigure support services for unaccompanied asylum-seeking children (Home Office, 2007b; Border and Immigration Agency, 2008) herald many changes with regard to case ownership, fast tracking of applications and dispersing children and young people to specialist authorities across England. These have important implications for how professionals and agencies within these specialist authorities are prepared and supported to work with the young people arriving within their care.

There are some key lessons from this study that might be used to facilitate this transition and which might encourage services to think creatively about how they can provide the best possible social and primary care, specialist health, education and legal services to young people within the resources available. Local authorities clearly need to develop specialist expertise in their work with unaccompanied asylum-seeking children and young people. They also need to consider how they can best offer the types of long-term support that young people clearly require in order to help them maintain a sense of well-being as they engage with complex legal, immigration, social care, education and welfare systems. This support may best be provided by a system of guardianship which would enable specialist and individual support to be provided to unaccompanied young people seeking asylum according to their individual needs.

# References

Achenbach T and Edelbrock C (1991) *Manual for the Child Behavior Checklist and Revised Child Behaviour Profile*, Texas: University Associates in Psychiatry

Armstrong C, Hill M and Secker J (2000) 'Young people's perceptions of mental health', *Children & Society* 14:1, pp 60–72

Bean T, Mooijaart A and Eurelings-Bontekoe P (2006) 'Validation of the child behavior checklist for guardians of unaccompanied refugee minors', *Children and Youth Services Review* 28:8, pp 867–87

Border and Immigration Agency (2008) *Better Outcomes: The way forward – improving the care of unaccompanied asylum-seeking children*, London: BIA

Buston K (2002) 'Adolescents with mental health problems: what do they say about mental health services?', *Journal of Adolescence* 25:2, pp 231–42

Cameron C, Bennert K, Simon A and Wigfall V (2007) *Using Health, Education, Housing and Other Services: A study of care leavers and young people in difficulty*, Research Briefing [online] www.dfes.gov.uk/research/data/uploadfiles/TCRU-01-07.pdf

Candappa M and Egharevba I (2000) *Extraordinary Childhoods: The social lives of refugee children*, Children 5–16 Research Briefing No 5, London: Economic and Social Research Council

Cheung R, Bemak F and Wong S (2000) 'Vietnamese refugees' levels of distress, social support and acculturation: implications for mental health counselling', *Journal of Mental Health Counselling* 22:2, pp 150–61

Crawley H (2007) *When is a Child not a Child? Asylum, age disputes and the process of age assessments*, London: Immigration Law Practitioners' Association

Davies J and Wright J (2008) 'Children's voices: a review of the literature pertinent to looked after children's views of mental health services', *Child and Adolescent Mental Health* 13:1, pp 26–31

Davies M and Webb E (2000) 'Promoting the psychological well-being of refugee children', *Clinical Child Psychology and Psychiatry* 5:4, pp 541–54

Dyregov A and Yule W (2006) 'A review of PTSD in Children', *Child and Adolescent Mental Health* 11:4, pp 176–84

Ehntholt K A and Yule W (2006) 'Assessment and treatment of refugee children and adolescents who have experienced war-related trauma', Practitioner review, *Journal of Child Psychology and Psychiatry* 47:12, pp 1197–210

Fazel M and Stein A (2003) 'Mental health of refugee children: a comparative study', *British Medical Journal* 327, 19 July

Foa E, Johnson K, Feeny N and Treadwell K (2001) 'The Child PTSD symptom scale: a preliminary examination of its psychometric properties', *Journal of Clinical Child Psychology* 30:3, pp 376–84

Frederick C, Pynoos R S and Nader K (1992) *Child Post-Traumatic Stress Disorder Reaction Index (CPTSD-RI)*, Los Angeles, CA: UCLA

Geltman P L, Grant-Knight W, Mehta S D and Lloyd C (2005) 'The lost boys of Sudan: functional and behavioral health of unaccompanied refugee minors resettled in the United States', *Archives of Pediatrics and Adolescent Medicine* 159:6, pp 585–91

Gibson R and Possami A (2002) 'What young people think about CAMHS', *Clinical Psychology* 18, pp 20–24

Gilligan R (2000) 'Adversity, resilience and young people: the protective value of positive school and spare time experiences', *Children & Society* 14:1, pp 37–47

Glaser B G and Strauss A L (1967) *The Discovery of Grounded Theory: Strategies for qualitative research*, Chicago: Aldine Publishing Company

Goodman R. (1997) 'The Strengths and Difficulties Questionnaire: a research note', *Journal of Child Psychology & Psychiatry* 38:5, pp 581–6

Green B, Koral M, Grace M, Vary M, Leonard A, Gleser G and Smitson-Cohen S (1991) 'Children and disaster: age, gender, and parental effects on PTSD symptoms', *Journal of the American Academy of Child & Adolescent Psychiatry* 30:6, pp 945–51

Harden A, Rees R, Shepherd J, Brunton G, Oliver S and Oakley A (2001) *Young People and Mental Health: A systematic review of research on barriers and facilitators*, London: EPPI-Centre, Institute of Education, University of London

Harris J and Oppenheimer D (2002) *Into the Arms of Strangers: Stories of the Kindertransport*, London: Bloomsbury Publishing

Hek R (2005a) *The Experiences and Needs of Refugee and Asylum Seeking Children in the UK: A literature review*, Research report 635, London: Department for Education and Skills

Hek R (2005b) 'The role of education in the settlement of young refugees in the UK: the experiences of young refugees', *Practice* 17:3, pp 157–71

Hodes M (1998) 'Refugee children may need a lot of psychiatric help', *British Medical Journal* 316, pp 793–94

Hodes M (2000) 'Psychologically distressed refugee children in the United Kingdom', *Child Psychology and Psychiatry Review* 5:2, pp 57–68

Hodes M (2002a) 'Implications for psychiatric services of chronic civilian strife: young refugees in the UK', *Advances in Psychiatric Treatment* 8, pp 366–74

Hodes M (2002b) 'Three key issues for young refugees' mental health', *Transcultural Psychiatry* 39:2, pp 196–213

Home Office (2006) *Asylum Statistics*, UASCs, 2006, London: Home Office

Home Office (2007a) *Asylum Statistics*, UASCs, Quarter 1, 2007, London: Home Office

Home Office (2007b) *Planning Better Outcomes and Support for Unaccompanied Asylum-Seeking Children*, London: Home Office

Hopkins P and Hill M (2006) *'This is a Good Place to Live and Think about the Future': The needs and experiences of unaccompanied asylum-seeking children and young people in Scotland*, Glasgow: Scottish Refugee Council

Horowitz M, Wilner N and Alvarez W (1979) 'Impact of event scale: a measure of subjective stress', *Psychosomatic Medicine* 41:3, pp 209–18

Hymen I, Vu N and Beiser M (2000) 'Post-migration stresses among Southeast Asian refugee youth in Canada: a research note', *Journal of Comparative Family Studies* 31:2, pp 281–93

Immigration Law Practitioners' Association (ILPA) (2007) *Children's Asylum Claims*, Information sheet 05 April 2007; available online at www.ilpa.org.uk/infoservice.html

Kidane S (2001) *Food, Shelter and Half a Chance: Assessing the needs of unaccompanied asylum seeking and refugee children*, London: BAAF

Kidane S and Amarena P (2004) *Fostering Unaccompanied Asylum Seeking and Refugee Children: A training course for foster carers*, London: BAAF

Kline P M and Mone E (2003) 'Coping with war: three strategies employed by adolescent citizens of Sierra Leone', *Child and Adolescent Social Work* 20:5, pp 321–33

Kohli R (2005) 'The sound of silence: listening to what unaccompanied asylum-seeking children say and do not say', *British Journal of Social Work* 36, pp 707–21

Kohli R K S and Mather R (2003) 'Promoting psychosocial well-being in unaccompanied asylum seeking young people in the United Kingdom', *Child & Family Social Work* 8:3, pp 201–12

Levenson R and Sharma A (1999) *The Health of Refugee Children: Guidelines for paediatricians*, London: Royal College of Paediatrics and Child Health

Leverton B and Lowensohn S (1990) *I Came Alone: The stories of the Kindertransports*, Brighton: The Book Guild Ltd

Marriott K (2001) *Living in Limbo: Young separated refugees in the West Midlands*, London: Save the Children

Melzak S and Avigad J (2005) *Thinking About Assessment of Asylum Seeker and Refugee Children Both Unaccompanied and Accompanied by Family Members*, London: Medical Foundation

Melzer H, Gatward R, Corbin T, Goodman R and Ford T (2003) *The Mental Health of Young People Looked After by Local Authorities in England*, London: The Stationery Office

Mental Health Foundation (2002) *The Mental Health of Looked After Children: Bright futures – working with vulnerable young people*, London: Mental Health Foundation

Merriam S B (2002) 'Assessing and evaluating qualitative research', in S B Merriam (ed) *Qualititative Research in Practice: Examples for discussion and analysis*, San Francisco, CA: Jossey-Bass

Newman E (2002) Assessment of PTSD and trauma exposure in adolescents, *Journal of Aggression, Maltreatment and Trauma* 6:1, pp 59–77

O'Dougherty Wright M and Marsten A (2006) 'Resilience processes in development: fostering positive adaptation in the context of adversity', in S Goldstein and R Brooks, *Handbook of Resilience in Children*, New York, NY: Springer

Porter M (2005) 'Predisplacement and postdisplacement factors associated with mental health of refugees and internally displaced persons', *Journal of the American Medical Association* 294, pp 602–12

Roose G and John A (2003) 'A focus group investigation into young children's understanding of mental health and their views on appropriate services for their age group', *Child: Care, Health and Development* 29:6, pp 545–50

Rose S, Bisson J and Wessely S (2003) 'A systematic review of single-session psychological interventions ("debriefing") following trauma', *Psychotherapy and Psychosomatics* 72, pp 176–84

Rousseau C, Said T, Gagné M and Bibeau G (1998) 'Resilience in unaccompanied minors from north of Somalia', *Psychoanalytical Review* 85:4, pp 615–63

Rutter J (2003) *Supporting Refugee Children in 21st Century Britain: A compendium of essential information*, Maidenhead: Open University Press

Rutter M (1985) 'Resilience in the face of adversity: protective factors and resistance to psychiatric disorder', *British Journal of Psychiatry* 147, pp 598–611

Rutter M (1987) 'Psychosocial resilience and protective mechanisms', *American Journal of Orthopsychiatry* 57:3, pp 316–31

Rutter M (1999) 'Resilience concepts and findings: implications for family therapy', *Journal of Family Therapy* 21, pp 119–44

Save the Children (2005) *Young Refugees: A guide to the rights and entitlements of separated refugee children*, London: Save the Children

Schofield G and Beek M (2005) 'Risk and resilience in long-term social care', *British Journal of Social Work* 35:8, pp 1283–301

Seale C (2002) 'Quality issues in qualitative inquiry', *Qualitative Social Work* 1, pp 97–110

Shaw J (2003) 'Children exposed to war/terrorism', *Clinical Child and Family Psychology Review* 6:4, pp 237–46

Sinclair I (2005) *Fostering Now: Messages from research*, London: Jessica Kingsley Publishers

Sourander A (1998) 'Behavior problems and traumatic events of unaccompanied refugee minors', *Child Abuse & Neglect* 22:7, pp 719–27

Spencer J and Le T (2006) 'Parent refugee status, immigration stressors and Southeast Asian youth violence', *Journal of Immigrant and Minority Health* 8:4, pp 359–68

Sporton D, Valentine G and Nielsen K (2006) 'Post conflict identities: affiliations and practices of Somali asylum seeker children', *Children's Geographies* 4:2, pp 203–17

Stanley K (2001) *Cold Comfort: Young separated refugees in England*, London: Save the Children

Street C (2004) *Mental Health Services: What children and young people want*, Highlight 210, London: National Children's Bureau

Street C, Stapelkamp C, Taylor E, Malek M and Kurtz Z (2005) *Minority Voices: Research into the access and acceptability of services for the mental health of young people from Black and minority ethnic groups*, London: Young Minds

Thomas S, Nafees B and Bhugr D (2004) '"I was running away from death" – the pre-flight experiences of unaccompanied asylum seeking children in the UK', *Child: Care, Health and Development* 20:2, pp 112–22

Tousignant M, Habimana E, Biron C and Malo C (1999) 'Quebec Adolescent Refugee Project: psychopathology and family variables in a sample from 35 nations', *Journal of American Academy of Child and Adolescent Psychiatry* 38, pp 1426–32

UNHCR (1992) *Handbook on Procedures and Criteria for Determining Refugee Status under the 1951 Convention and the 1967 Protocol Relating to the Status of Refugees*, Geneva: UNHCR

UNHCR (1994) *Refugee Children: Guidelines on protection and care*, Geneva: UNHCR

USA Public Health Service (2000) *Mental Health: A report of the Surgeon General* [online], www.surgeongeneral.gov/library/mentalhealth/chapter8/ref8.html; accessed 6 December 2005

Vostanis P (2004) 'My practice', *Community Care*, 7 October

Vostanis P (2005) 'Meeting the mental health needs of young people leaving care: strategies and challenges', in B Broad, *Improving the Health and Well Being of Young People Leaving Care*, Lyme Regis: Russell House Publishing

Wade J, Mitchell F and Baylis G (2005) *Unaccompanied Asylum Seeking Children: The response of social work services*, London: BAAF

Wallin A and Ahlstrom G (2005) 'Unaccompanied young adult refugees in Sweden, experiences of their life situation and well-being: a qualitative follow-up study', *Ethnicity and Health* 10:2, pp 129–44

Ward H, Jones H, Lynch M and Skuse T (2002) 'Issues concerning the health of looked after children', *Adoption & Fostering* 26:4, pp 8–18

Whittaker S, Hardy G, Lewis K and Buchan L (2005) 'An exploration of psychological well-being with young Somali refugee and asylum seeker women', *Clinical Child Psychology & Psychiatry* 10:2, pp 177–96

World Health Organisation (1978) *Declaration of Alma Alta*, Geneva: WHO

# Appendix
## Study participants

| Name | Gender | Country of origin | Age upon arrival in the UK | Age at the time of the study |
|------|--------|-------------------|---------------------------|------------------------------|
| Ajani | Male | Afghanistan | 14 | 18 |
| Alban | Male | Albania | 15 | 20 |
| Ali | Male | Afghanistan | 13 | 15 |
| Aliya | Female | Somalia | 17 | 21 |
| Amir | Male | Iran | 16 | 18 |
| Asif | Male | Afghanistan | 10 | 15 |
| Azyeb | Female | Eritrea | 12 | 18 |
| Betania | Female | Angola | 16 | 18 |
| Chrisna | Female | DRC | 15 | 18 |
| Christiana | Female | Nigeria | 15 | 18 |
| Claude | Male | Burundi | 15 | 18 |
| Daisy | Female | China | 16 | 21 |
| Faith | Female | Nigeria | 15 | 17 |
| Hellen | Female | Ethiopia | 15 | 17 |
| Houmam | Male | Syria | 15 | 16 |
| Hossain | Male | Afghanistan | 12 | 15 |
| Ibrahim | Male | Pakistan | 16 | 19 |
| Innocent | Male | Nigeria | 16 | 20 |
| Joy | Female | Nigeria | 13 | 17 |
| Kenneh | Male | Liberia | 13 | 17 |
| Kiki | Female | Eritrea | 15 | 15 |
| Lee | Female | China | 16 | 21 |
| Mahamat | Male | Chad | 17 | 23 |
| Mahlet | Female | Ethiopia | 14 | 16 |
| Malashu | Female | Eritrea | 15 | 17 |
| Maryam | Female | Iran | 17 | 21 |
| Mesaret | Female | Ethiopia | 16 | 18 |
| Miguel | Male | Angola | 12 | 18 |
| Mireille | Female | Cameroon | 16 | 18 |
| Nadine | Female | Rwanda | 15 | 19 |

| Naeema  | Female | Eritrea     | 16 | 18 |
|---------|--------|-------------|----|----|
| Namir   | Male   | Afghanistan | 9  | 11 |
| Nancy   | Female | China       | 17 | 19 |
| Nanu    | Female | Eritrea     | 16 | 20 |
| Nasir   | Male   | Somalia     | 17 | 18 |
| Patrick | Male   | DRC         | 12 | 15 |
| Peter   | Male   | Uganda      | 13 | 18 |
| Rakeb   | Female | Eritrea     | 15 | 21 |
| Remi    | Female | Nigeria     | 14 | 16 |
| Ruth    | Female | Eritrea     | 12 | 13 |
| Saba    | Female | Eritrea     | 12 | 14 |
| Samuel  | Male   | Eritrea     | 16 | 23 |
| Sebel   | Female | Ethiopia    | 16 | 18 |
| Sheriff | Male   | Liberia     | 16 | 21 |
| Simeon  | Male   | Somalia     | 13 | 20 |
| Thierry | Male   | Burundi     | 13 | 16 |
| William | Male   | DRC         | 17 | 19 |
| Wini    | Female | Eritrea     | 16 | 20 |
| Yang    | Female | China       | 16 | 18 |
| Yasir   | Male   | Afghanistan | 13 | 18 |
| Yemi    | Female | Nigeria     | 14 | 16 |
| Zalmai  | Male   | Afghanistan | 11 | 13 |
| Zelgai  | Male   | Afghanistan | 9  | 11 |
| Zemar   | Male   | Afghanistan | 16 | 20 |

# Also available from BAAF

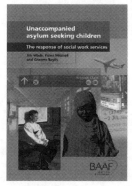

## Unaccompanied asylum-seeking children
### The response of social work services
*Jim Wade, Fiona Mitchell and Graeme Baylis*

'This book is an essential read, equally for those who are well versed with this area of social care, as well as those who are new to it. It is highly thought-provoking, and provides an inclusive critique of the complex circumstances of young people seeking asylum and what might constitute the most appropriate and effective social work response.'
*Elaine Chase, Thomas Coram Research Unit*

The displacement of unaccompanied young people to countries far from home happens for many reasons, from the need to seek safety from armed conflict or natural disasters, to the desperate escape from deprivation or exploitation by traffickers. What unites these young people is the experience of being separated from their families, uprooted from their homes and divided from their culture and all that is familiar.

This ground-breaking study examines key questions including:
- How do social work services in the UK respond to young asylum seekers?
- Are asylum seeking children entitled to the same service as looked after children and, if so, do they receive it?
- How are young people's needs defined and assessed?
- How do the services provided affect their progress and welfare?

Illustrated by numerous comments from team managers and social workers, as well as children and young people, this illuminating study will prove invaluable to childcare professionals, asylum teams, those involved with refugee communities, teachers and students.

BAAF NOVEMBER 2005    248 PAGES A5    ISBN 1 903699 86 X    £12.95

Order online at www.baaf.org.uk or by phoning
BAAF Publications on 020 7421 2604 or emailing
pubs.sales@baaf.org.uk

*British Association for Adoption and Fostering is a registered charity no. 275689 (England and Wales) and SC039337 (Scotland)*